The Translator and Editor

SHEILA MURNAGHAN is the Alfred Reginald Allen Memorial Professor of Greek at the University of Pennsylvania. She is the author of *Disguise and Recognition in the Odyssey* and numerous articles on Greek epic and tragedy, gender in classical culture, and classical reception. She is the co-editor of *Odyssean Identities in Modern Cultures: The Journey Home* and *Women and Slaves in Classical Culture: Differential Equations*.

NORTON CRITICAL EDITIONS
ANCIENT, CLASSICAL, AND MEDIEVAL ERAS

For a complete list of Norton Critical Editions, visit
wwnorton.com/nortoncriticals

A NORTON CRITICAL EDITION

Euripides
MEDEA

A NEW TRANSLATION
CONTEXTS
CRITICISM

Translated and Edited by

SHEILA MURNAGHAN
UNIVERSITY OF PENNSYLVANIA

W · W · NORTON & COMPANY · *New York* · *London*

W. W. Norton & Company has been independent since its founding in 1923, when William Warder Norton and Mary D. Herter Norton first published lectures delivered at the People's Institute, the adult education division of New York City's Cooper Union. The Nortons soon expanded their program beyond the Institute, publishing books by celebrated academics from America and abroad. By mid-century, the two major pillars of Norton's publishing program—trade books and college texts—were firmly established. In the 1950s, the Norton family transferred control of the company to its employees, and today—with a staff of 400 and a comparable number of trade, college, and professional titles published each year—W. W. Norton & Company stands as the largest and oldest publishing house owned wholly by its employees.

Library of Congress Cataloging-in-Publication Data

Names: Euripides, author. | Murnaghan, Sheila, 1951– translator, editor.
Title: Medea : a new translation, contexts, criticism / Euripides ; translated and
    edited by Sheila Murnaghan.
Other titles: Medea. English (Murnaghan) | Norton critical edition.
Description: First edition. | New York ; London : W. W. Norton & Company,
    2018. | Series: A Norton critical edition | Includes bibliographical references.
Identifiers: LCCN 2017048510 | ISBN 9780393265453 (pbk.)
Subjects: LCSH: Medea, consort of Aegeus, King of Athens (Mythological
    character)—Drama. | LCGFT: Drama. | Tragedies (Drama)
Classification: LCC PA3975.M4 M77 2018 | DDC 882/.01—dc23
    LC record available at https://lccn.loc.gov/2017048510

W. W. Norton & Company, Inc., 500 Fifth Avenue, New York, NY 10110
wwnorton.com

W. W. Norton & Company, Inc., 15 Carlisle Street, London W1D 3BS

1 2 3 4 5 6 7 8 9 0

For Stanley Lombardo

Contents

Introduction

How can a mother willingly kill her own children? That question haunts Euripides' *Medea* and has shaped hundreds of retellings of the Medea story since the play was first produced at the Festival of Dionysus in Athens in 431 B.C.E. Like all tragic playwrights of his time, Euripides was dramatizing a longstanding, well-known myth. But he was also free to reinvent its details, and his audience would have been eager to see what twist he was giving to a generally familiar course of events. It is likely (although not certain) that Medea's deliberate killing of her two sons was Euripides' innovation. The possibility that she might harm them is raised in ominously vague terms in the prologue, as Medea's Nurse sets the scene for this new version of the story: Medea, in a state of wounded outrage at being abandoned by her husband Jason, is unmoved by her children: "She hates her sons, gets no joy from seeing them. / I am afraid that she is planning something" (lines 36–37). As the plot unfolds and Medea's plans take shape, that "something" turns out to be a course of revenge that destroys Jason's new wife, the bride's father (the king of Corinth, where the family is living), and finally the children.

Medea carries out an act that people routinely reject as inhuman and incomprehensible—beginning with her stunned victim Jason, who sees Medea revealed as an animal or a monster—even though mothers have often purposefully killed their children under various circumstances throughout recorded history (see pages 62–63 and 94–95). By dramatizing the sequence of events that leads up to Medea's infanticide, Euripides shows how such a supposedly unthinkable thing can happen and challenges his audience to recognize its roots in familiar features of their own world. He provides a thrilling, terrifying portrait of a woman of exceptional powers and unyielding vengefulness, but her interactions throughout the play make it clear how normal she can appear and how much she has in common with ordinary women; she acts in response to circumstances of which she is herself a victim and that stem from the routine arrangements of classical Greek society and from unremarkable acts of blindness and selfishness on the part of others.

Medea is typical of many classical Athenian tragedies in that it focuses on shocking and transgressive events, especially violence between people bound by ties of kinship, and makes them believable. But Euripides characteristically does less than the other surviving tragedians to suggest that such events, however disturbing to their human witnesses, can be understood within a broader cosmic frame. Many characters in *Medea* call on the traditional Greek gods to notice their sufferings and make sure that justice is done, but there is no discernible divine response to Medea's actions. The play leaves its audience to find its own ways to make sense of the unthinkable as they confront forms of suffering that seem to exceed reasonable expectation and are commonly labeled "tragic."

The Myth before Euripides

Medea and Jason are central characters in the Argonaut legend, already described as "well-known to all" in Homer's *Odyssey*, one of our earliest Greek texts (probably dating to the 700's b.c.e. and incorporating much older material).[1] We have no complete account that is earlier than Euripides, but we can piece together the basic contours of the traditional myth and some of its more variable features from brief references, fragments of lost works, depictions in vase painting, and later versions.

The hero Jason is sent out by his uncle Pelias from the Greek city of Iolcus (now known as Volos) on a dangerous mission to bring back the Golden Fleece—the prized pelt of a magical winged ram—from the kingdom of Colchis on the far shores of the Black Sea (modern-day Georgia). Pelias has usurped the power of Jason's father and is hoping to get rid of an inconvenient heir to the throne by presenting him with this challenge. Jason commissions a ship, the *Argo*, and assembles a group of companions, known as the Argonauts. Together they sail to Colchis, where they encounter King Aeetes, son of the sun-god Helios, and his daughter Medea. Aeetes sets an impossible task as the price of the fleece: Jason must yoke together two fire-breathing bulls, then plow a field and sow it with dragon's teeth (which produces a crop of ferocious armed warriors). But Medea falls in love with Jason (through the intervention of his divine patron Hera, wife of Zeus, and Aphrodite, the goddess of love), and she gives him a magic potion that allows him to withstand the bulls, then helps him defeat the sown men and overcome the huge serpent or dragon who guards the fleece. As Jason and Medea escape together with the fleece, her father Aeetes pursues them, but she devises a grisly way of slowing him down: she kills her brother Apsyrtus and tosses out pieces of his body, which Aeetes stops to gather for burial. Back in Iolcus, Medea helps Jason take an equally gruesome revenge on

---

1. Homer, *Odyssey* 12.70.

Pelias. She uses her magical powers to rejuvenate a ram by chopping it into pieces and boiling it in a cauldron, then convinces Pelias's daughters to try the same procedure on him. In a variant on this motif, Medea in some versions genuinely rejuvenates Jason's old father Aeson.

After Medea's time in Iolcus, her story continues in two other Greek cities. The first is Corinth, to which in some accounts she has a genealogical connection through her father, who had migrated from Greece to Colchis. There her children die: in some versions she kills them inadvertently; in others they are killed by the Corinthians, who are angry at some sort of attack on the royal family. From Corinth, Medea travels to Athens and marries King Aegeus. This makes her the stepmother of his son Theseus, who has been raised elsewhere by his mother. When Theseus arrives unannounced in Athens, she persuades Aegeus to send him into exile or to poison him, but he is eventually recognized as his father's son and rescued from her plots.

The fullest version that predates Euripides comes in an ode by the lyric poet Pindar written in honor of Arcesilas, an aristocrat who traced his ancestry to one of the Argonauts, around forty years before Euripides' *Medea*. Pindar mixes praise for Arcesilas with a selective account of the myth, focusing on Jason and Pelias in Iolcus; on the voyage to Colchis; on Aphrodite's use of love magic to help Jason seduce Medea "so that he might take away her respect for her parents"; on Jason's success in gaining the fleece with the help of Medea's concoctions and his abduction of "Medea the future killer of Pelias";[2] and on a prophecy delivered by Medea to Arcesilas's ancestor during the journey back to Greece. A number of tragedies that are now lost focused on particular sections of the myth. Sophocles wrote three plays concerning the events in Colchis and the return voyage. In one of his first plays, *The Daughters of Pelias*, produced in 455, Euripides dramatized the murder that Pindar refers to, and both Sophocles and Euripides wrote plays with the title *Aegeus* about the last, Athenian phase of the myth.[3]

From what we can tell, then, the audience of Euripides' *Medea* would have known Medea as a foreign princess, the granddaughter of the sun-god, skilled in the use of magical herbs and potions and gifted with prophecy, motivated by love and capable of betraying her family and committing strategic murders—but probably not as the killer of her own children.

2. Pindar, *Pythian Odes* 4.218, 250.
3. We have some scattered, inconclusive evidence about a *Medea* by another tragedian, Neophron, a contemporary of Euripides whose works are all now lost. This was so close to Euripides' version in several details, including Medea's willful killing of the children, that some ancient scholars claimed Euripides had copied it; modern scholars generally conclude the opposite, that the play in question was influenced by Euripides. See Mastronarde pp. 57–64.

The Context of Euripides' Version

Euripides' play was presented as part of a competition among tragic playwrights at the Festival of Dionysus, a divinity associated with wine, madness, revelry, and the theater, held in Athens every spring. This festival was a religious and political occasion, on which the city worshipped one of the major Olympian gods while also celebrating its own achievements and showing them off to visiting foreigners. In addition to drama and other kinds of poetic performance, the festival included a procession and animal sacrifice dedicated to the god, displays of financial tribute from Athens' allies, a parade of orphaned sons of men who had died fighting for the city, and the ceremonial crowning of prominent citizens.

It was typical of the Greeks to honor their gods by staging competitions in which they showed off their athletic and artistic abilities, and tragedy was a cultural achievement of which Athens was especially proud. It was at Athens, beginning in the late sixth century B.C.E., that a type of choral poetry performed by a group of singers and dancers was gradually transformed, through the addition of individual actors, into drama. In tragedy, traditional myths were acted out instead of being narrated by the chorus, which was incorporated into the story as a group of interested bystanders. Many tragic plots centered on the most violent and disturbing episodes in those myths, such as Medea's murder of her children, and those events were generally not presented directly. But the tragedians developed resources for bringing offstage occurrences to life, including vivid and detailed reports by messengers. These messengers' speeches were just one element in a spectacular multimedia performance—including spoken dialogue, choral song and dance, lyric passages sung by individual actors, and vivid costumes and scenery—that was widely admired throughout the Greek world.

Athens in 431 had a prominent place within the network of city-states that made up the Greek world. These were politically independent communities bound together by a common language and culture and involved in complex, ever-shifting alliances. Over the preceding century, the Athenians had adopted a democratic form of government and an active role in foreign affairs: they took the lead in warding off the Persians, possessors of a large and expanding empire to the east, who had invaded Greece in 490 and again in 480. In the years that followed, Athens continued to grow as a naval and sea-trading power, especially under the leadership of Pericles, a charismatic, aristocratic politician. The league formed to fight the Persians was gradually transformed into a power base that was itself a kind of empire. The city was famous for its intellectual and artistic achievements, including tragedy, comedy, and other forms of poetry, and had recently, in 438, dedicated a magnificent new temple, the Parthenon, to its patron goddess Athena. But Athens' rapidly growing power and autocratic treatment of its allies created tensions, especially with such major cities as Corinth, Thebes, and Sparta. Only a few weeks after the first performance of *Medea*, the Peloponnesian War broke out between Athens and its allies and Sparta and its allies. The War continued off and on for several decades, leaving the city drained and demoralized and finally ending with the defeat of Athens in 404—a major blow, but not the end of Athens' role as an important political and intellectual center.

The Mythic and the Ordinary

Tragedy was very much the product of fifth-century Athens, but the events dramatized in the plays belong to the legendary past and occur mostly in other places, such as Troy, Thebes, or (as in *Medea*) Corinth. As a result, there is a protective gap between the abhorrent and disruptive events of tragic plots and the city that showcased its own success by dramatizing them; when Athens figures in tragic scenarios, it is usually as an enlightened haven for struggling outsiders. But this popular, culturally central genre could also be a medium for addressing contemporary issues, offering a distant mirror for the audience's own world.

Among the three major tragedians, Euripides was seen by his contemporaries as going further than Aeschylus or Sophocles in making figures from heroic legends resemble modern Athenians in their patterns of speech and their concerns. His plays reflect the intellectual currents of the late fifth century, especially the ideas of a controversial group of thinkers known as the Sophists, who raised fundamental questions about the validity of social conventions and religious traditions and stressed the power of human reasoning and argumentation as the basis of belief. Many Sophists were teachers of the rhetorical skills that were essential to Athenian public life, in which major political decisions were made in a popular assembly and the law courts were also an important arena of personal advancement. Although he undoubtedly calls many received truths into question, Euripides cannot be easily aligned with or against the Sophists, but we see the impact of their thought—and of Athens' rhetorical culture—throughout *Medea*. It surfaces in the characters' observations about the advantages and limits of cleverness and the effects of skillful speech, and especially in the long central debate between Medea and Jason over the rights and wrongs of their marriage, in which Jason in particular makes a number of ingenious but also dubious arguments (465–575).

The situation that Medea and Jason argue about has its origins in far-flung travel and supernatural adventures. In setting the scene,

Medea's Nurse begins with Jason's fateful passage through the Clash-ing Rocks, the perilous, otherworldly barrier that marks the entrance to the Black Sea and represents a dividing line between the Greek world and the foreign territory outside it. But she is soon describing his and Medea's return to Greece and speaking in general terms about a wife's loyalty to her husband as the best safeguard for a mar-riage: the conflict between husband and wife that plays out in Corinth exposes the fault lines in a familiar institution at the heart of fifth-century Athenian society. Medea has been brought to Greece from a distant Asiatic home, but the relationship between her foreign status and what she does in the course of the play is by no means straightfor-ward, complicating rather than affirming contemporary Athenian ideas about foreigners.

Mid-fifth-century Athens was marked by tensions around ques-tions of ethnic identity and the integration of foreigners. The war against Persia at the beginning of the century had solidified ideas of Greek identity and especially of Greek superiority to non-Greeks, who were variously portrayed as slavish, luxury-loving, treacherous, law-less, and overly passionate; as the leaders of that struggle, the Athe-nians saw themselves as the chief defenders of Greek values. The distinction between Athenians and others was also reinforced by a law passed in 451 that restricted the much-prized rights of citizenship to children with an Athenian mother as well as an Athenian father.

We hear echoes of contemporary attitudes in Medea's pointed observation that Jason is abandoning her because he thinks a foreign wife will become an embarrassment (591–92) and in Jason's outburst when he learns of the children's murder: "No Greek woman would ever do that" (1339). That is an understandable reaction from a devas-tated victim, but many aspects of Medea and Jason's story tell against the idea that she is more like a conventional foreigner than he is. It is Jason who is conspicuously guilty of treachery. As the chorus of Corinthian women points out, Medea crossed over to the Greek world "[b]ecause of an oath" (210) overseen by Themis, the goddess associ-ated with justice and proper order—the oath being an important Greek cultural norm that Jason has violated. When Jason claims dur-ing their debate that Medea has gained the most from their relation-ship because she now lives in Greece, where she benefits from justice and the rule of law (534–44), those patriotic claims ring hollow.

When Medea first appears on stage, emerging from her house to make contact with the chorus, she offers an analysis of marriage in which every wife is in essence a foreigner:

> Finding herself among strange laws and customs,
> a wife needs to be clairvoyant; she hasn't
> learned at home how to deal with her mate. (238–40)

Medea's description of marriage is colored by unhappy experience, but its features correspond to the contemporary institution that Euripides' audience would have known. Marriage in fifth-century Athens was a transaction between male-headed households, in which a woman left her father's house and entered into the house of her husband. There her life was spent mostly inside and her most important function was child-bearing. Ideally (as in the passage from Xenophon's *Oeconomicus* that appears in this Norton Critical Edition), this was a harmonious, respectful division of labor, with each spouse pursuing the couple's shared interests in a different sphere, the husband tending to business outside the house and the wife working inside under his protection. But the prime beneficiaries of classical marriages were undoubtedly the men who arranged and controlled them: the fathers who cemented their relations with other men by giving them their daughters and the husbands who gained a means of producing heirs for their families. Although Jason's situation as an outsider advancing himself through a royal marriage also evokes a distant world, his freedom to abandon Medea when expedient is in line with Athenian law, which granted men but not women the right to divorce at will.

Medea's bitter words reveal how asymmetrical this arrangement might seem to a woman: largely confined to the house, a woman has nowhere to turn if she is lonely or unhappy, while a man can go out and find other company; men's efforts in the outside world, especially as soldiers, are more highly valued than the taxing labor of childbirth.

Fictional tragic heroines become visible and speak in a public context as real classical Athenian women did not, and Medea's unusual powers and history put her in a position to articulate and act on feelings that were not usually aired but may well have been widely experienced. The conviction that her husband ought to protect her interests, which fuels Medea's anger at Jason, reflects what any wife might justly expect, a point that Euripides makes through his use of the chorus. Every new tragedy involved the playwright in a decision about what identity to assign the chorus, a collective character whose relation to the action was usually that of an observer or bystander (although not necessarily a model for the audience) and whose songs combined the particular outlook of its fictional identity with traditional communal values. In *Medea*, Euripides chose to pair his exceptional female protagonist with a group of women who also claim an unexpected voice for themselves but are clearly identified as ordinary Corinthians. Their sympathy for Medea's grievances and support for her plans to punish Jason effectively affirm the broad relevance of her complaints.

Medea's Divided Self

Medea establishes a strong connection with the chorus, but she is not actually herself an ordinary woman. She makes her case so compellingly that it is easy to forget the darker details of her past and the wilder aspects of her personality. When she tells them that she is worse off than they are because she has "no mother, brother, or other family / to shelter me now that disaster has struck" (257–58), she elides the fact that she willingly betrayed her father when she left home with Jason, chopping her brother into pieces as she went. Her Nurse, the person who knows her best, has already mentioned her next exploit, persuading the daughters of Pelias to kill their father, and has also given some ominous hints about her nature, introducing the comparisons between Medea and wild animals or harsh natural elements like rocks and the sea that recur throughout the play. Medea's cries from behind the stage, when she has not yet assumed her public persona, reveal something of the depth and extremity of the emotions that drive her.

Medea's exceptional nature is most fully realized in her willingness to pursue revenge to a point where the chorus can no longer follow her with sympathy or comprehension: the killing of her own children. This difference springs not from her foreignness so much as from her investment in a set of attitudes and values typically associated with Greek men: she presents a mixture of qualities that unsettle the categories of male and female as well as the categories of Greek and non-Greek. In contracting her own marriage, she has taken upon herself a prerogative that would normally belong to her father, and she treats her arrangement with Jason as if it were a pact between two men. In particular, she portrays their marriage as an agreement secured by solemn oaths of a kind found in the male spheres of public and social life; even before she appears, we hear from the Nurse that she is "shouting about their oaths" (21). In this way, she appeals to one of the most sacred customs of the Greek world: oaths were sworn by invoking the gods, who were believed to punish those who broke them, and this fortifies her in her confidence that she is acting as a righteous, divinely backed avenger. As many critics have pointed out, Medea's determination and sense of injustice also make her more like some of the male heroes encountered in the Homeric epics and other tragedies (for example, Achilles in the *Iliad* and Ajax in Sophocles' *Ajax*) than like a conventional female character. In common with those heroes, she has a robust sense of her own honor, which she will go to any lengths to protect, and is particularly enraged by the thought that her enemies might be laughing at her.

Medea may have the tenacity and self-regard of a male hero, but she carries out her revenge by drawing on the resources of a woman—and an ordinary woman, not a divinely connected sorcer-ess or an exotic foreigner. One of these is the deadly poison that she uses on Jason's new wife. Athenian women of the classical period were regularly suspected of resorting to poison. In a speech that sur-vives from a fourth-century court case, for example, a man accuses his stepmother of killing his father by arranging for a deadly potion to be introduced into his after-dinner wine.[4]

Medea relies heavily on her cleverness (a trait that she and others bring up repeatedly) and especially her gift for persuasion, qualities that Greek men often attributed to women and feared in them. The brilliant performances with which she draws others to her cause make her like an actor or a stage manager, and this connects her portrayal to contemporary concerns about the deceptiveness and emotional power of the theater, which was sometimes seen as a dan-gerously feminine medium. The opening exchange in which she convinces the chorus to keep quiet about her plans is only the first of a series of encounters in which Medea manipulates other people for her own ends. She talks Creon into letting her stay in Corinth just long enough that she can carry out her revenge; she gets the King of Athens, Aegeus, to agree to take her in after she leaves Corinth; and she convinces Jason that she accepts his new marriage, with the result that he helps her send lethal gifts to his new wife.

Medea's most effective means of hurting Jason is rooted in the capacity to bear children, for which women were at once valued and resented in the patriarchal world of classical Greece. For Athenians, in particular, the importance of motherhood was accentuated by the citizenship law of 451, which made having an Athenian mother a nec-essary qualification for citizenship. Medea skillfully exploits men's dependence on women for the offspring they want and need. She overcomes Aegeus's misgivings by promising to use her skill with drugs to solve his ongoing childlessness. And she cuts off all of Jason's hopes by killing not only his existing children but also his second wife who, as he callously points out, could give him new ones.

Even as she internalizes male values and treats her feminine qual-ities as useful tools, Medea remains a mother with a powerful attachment to her sons. The chorus's ability to identify with her breaks down when they realize that she really intends to kill the boys. This is due in part to their horror at so momentous a violation of human and divine law, but also to the fact that she is taking a step that is bound to make her "impossibly wretched" (818). Yet Medea's resolve to go through with the infanticide does not mean that she ever stops feeling a mother's pain at the loss she is inflicting on her-self as well as Jason. This becomes clear in the remarkable extended

4. Antiphon 1, "On the Stepmother."

monologue in which she wrestles with her decision; in that speech, she reveals a painfully divided self, torn between her drive for vengeance and her maternal feelings and so (as the discussion by Helene Foley in this Norton Critical Edition shows in detail) between the masculine and feminine sides of her character.

Jason's instinctive response to Medea's infanticide is to call her an animal and a freak, "an inhuman wife, a lioness / more savage than Etruscan Scylla" (1342–43). But what Medea does is more disturbing than Jason's labels can express because it arises so naturally out of circumstances and feelings that may take unusual and exaggerated forms but are fundamentally familiar and human (as discussed in the essay by P. E. Easterling in this Norton Critical Edition). Unlike many later retellers of her story, Euripides insists that, even if what Medea does is abhorrent, she remains entirely sane, consciously in control of her actions and recognizably the same woman who appeared at the play's opening as a justly aggrieved victim of mistreatment.

Only at the very end of the play is Medea revealed as a superhuman figure, through a stunning theatrical effect. Hearing the news of his children's death, Jason has rushed to the house and is banging on the door. This is the same door through which the audience saw Medea enter when her mind was finally made up and through which they heard the terrified cries of the trapped boys, and they would have expected that door to open and a wheeled platform to come out, bringing the bloody scene inside into view. But suddenly Medea is heard speaking from high above, at the top of the house, lifted up by a special crane to a position normally occupied by actors playing gods. She stands in a magic chariot drawn by dragons and sent by her grandfather the Sun.

As Medea looks down on Jason, belittling his efforts and reveling in her invulnerability, she exhibits the arrogance and indifference to human suffering of which the Greek gods are capable, a theme explored in many of Euripides' plays. As she and Jason spar for the last time, he is hopelessly outmatched and sadly diminished, punished in a way that is out of proportion with his shallow, thoughtless, self-seeking behavior. Gods like Zeus and Themis, who uphold justice and good order and who have been repeatedly invoked throughout the play, are absent from this ending, apparently willing to see Medea escape unpunished. This disturbing outcome is compounded by Medea's destination: in a travesty of the city's traditional role as a safe haven for powerless outcasts, Athens will take in and protect the mother who brought herself to kill her own children.

A New Song for Women?

Jason's abandonment of Medea inspires the chorus to sing about the one-sidedness of the poetic tradition, which abounds in stories of treacherous women, but only because they are produced by men.

> Enough of ancient poets' legends
> that tell of us as breaking faith!
> The lord of song, divine Apollo,
> did not grant the lyre's sweet music
> for the speaking of our minds,
> or I could have made an answer
> to the stories spread by men.
> Time's long record speaks on both sides. (421–31)

These women use the voice they gain as figures in a tragic plot to imagine a different kind of song, one that would tell women's side of the story. This raises the question of whether we should see Euripides' play, with its focus on an articulate woman whose life has been ruined by her husband's exercise of male privilege, as such a song. Certainly Medea's opening speech gives a memorable analysis of the disadvantages to women of patriarchal marriage. Both Creon and Jason see her through a misogynistic lens, attributing to her the stereotypical female qualities of emotional excess, sexual obsession, and deviousness. Jason's frustration at her refusal to support his plans culminates in a generalized wish that men would not have to deal with women at all:

> We should have some other way of getting children.
> Then there would be no female race,
> and mankind would be free from trouble. (573–75)

Medea deftly exploits these attitudes to achieve her goals. She appeals to Creon and Aegeus with displays of weepy helplessness, and persuades Jason to excuse her earlier anger with a brilliantly tentative reference to female weakness:

> Women just are . . . well, not quite wicked,
> but anyway you shouldn't copy us
> and get caught up in silly quarrels. (889–91)

But *Medea* is a play, not a manifesto, and no character can be simply identified as speaking for the author. The wrongs that Medea has suffered call forth remarkably direct statements about the power imbalance that makes them possible. But she answers them with passionate acts of vengeance that are so vicious and so deeply destructive of the innocent as well as the guilty that they overwhelm the structural unfairness of Athenian gender arrangements. In the end, the play tells a story of devastating female treachery, and Medea herself, as she summons the strength to carry out her plan, voices a darkly self-hating view of women:

> Now Medea, use everything you know; . . .
> You have the skill, and along with that
> a woman's nature—useless for doing good
> but just right for contriving evil. (401, 407–409)

It is not really possible to generalize about Euripides' view of women; in antiquity his unusually intimate portraits of women's emotional lives earned him a reputation both for a kind of proto-feminism and for misogyny (partly on the grounds that he hurt women by revealing their secrets). His interest in female psychology went together with a tendency to portray women as the first point of entry for dangerous passions that could spread through a community and undermine all of its meaningful distinctions. The play clearly raises issues that its audience needed to think about, and it might be helpful to know whether women were part of that audience. But our evidence for that question, which consists largely of scattered anecdotes, is inconclusive. We can only be sure that tragedy, which was composed by men and performed by men, presented its challenging scenarios to the city's male citizens, and we can only speculate about the lessons they drew from it.

The Afterlife of Medea

Euripides' play represents an especially influential chapter in the long and varied tradition of the Medea myth, which is still evolving in the twenty-first century, with frequent productions and new adaptations. The further retellings that survive from the classical world build on Euripides' interest in the psychology of a woman under extreme pressure and struggling with conflicting impulses. The most significant treatment by a later Greek author comes in the *Argonautica* by Apollonius of Rhodes, an epic narrative of the Argonauts' journey to Colchis written in the third century B.C.E. (and excerpted in this Norton Critical Edition). Unlike the earlier epics of the Homeric period, the *Argonautica* focuses on romantic love as much as heroic adventure, and one of its four books is devoted to an extensive portrait of Medea as a young woman in her father's house torn between her love for Jason and her duty as a daughter.

Medea was the subject of numerous plays by Roman authors writing in Latin, most of which are now lost. One of those was by the poet Ovid (43 B.C.E.–17 C.E.), who also treated Medea in his surviving mythological epic, the *Metamorphoses*. Like Apollonius, Ovid dwells particularly on Medea's first steps on the path of evil, depicting her inner turmoil as she debates whether to cast her lot with Jason, until she finally decides to do what she knows is wrong, fully aware that she has been undone by love. A half century later Seneca (4 B.C.E.–65 C.E.) wrote a *Medea* that closely follows Euripides' plot, but gives it a more sensational treatment (an excerpt appears in this Norton Critical Edition). Seneca fully develops those sides of Medea that Euripides plays down or balances with competing qualities. His Medea is a bloodthirsty seeker of vengeance from the outset, a more willing pursuer of evil, and a true witch.

While Seneca's version, like his other tragedies, had an important influence on revivals of Greek tragedy from the Renaissance on, most modern versions of the myth move in the opposite direction, finding some way to make Medea's child-killing more understandable and acceptable in human terms. A version by Richard Glover performed in London in 1767 adopts a strategy that may have been present in some pre-Euripidean variants, portraying Medea as the victim of temporary madness or "phrenzy." Over the last two centuries, many writers have responded to the possibility of making Medea a clear figure for marginalized people, whether as a woman or as a foreigner. In nineteenth-century England, her famous speech on the hard lot of wives was recited at meetings of suffragettes. Medea and Jason's different origins have been variously reconceived as differences of culture and race. To give only a few examples out of many, Medea has been reenvisioned as a princess from a fictional Asian country married to a French colonial administrator (Henri Lenormand, *Asie*, 1931), as a black African bride brought home to Puritan New England by her seafaring husband (Maxwell Anderson, *The Wingless Victory*, 1936), and as an Irish traveler treated as an outcast by her well-established in-laws (Marina Carr, *By the Bog of Cats*, 1998). In Pier Paolo Pasolini's 1969 film starring Maria Callas, Medea belongs to a primitive world in close harmony with nature and divinity, while Jason represents industrialized, bourgeois modern society.

This conception of Medea as an outsider is often accompanied by the idea that she kills her children for their own good, to spare them an even worse fate (an idea that emerges in Euripides, but only after Medea has herself sealed their fate by making them the agents of her attack on Jason's new wife). This was the case with Margaret Garner, a real woman who came to be known as "the modern Medea." Garner was an escaped slave in pre–Civil War America who, when apprehended by U.S. Marshals, killed her daughter to prevent her from being returned to slavery; her story became the basis of Toni Morrison's 1987 novel *Beloved*. In Guy Butler's *Demea* (written in the 1960s but first performed in 1990) a black South African Medea figure kills her children to save them from apartheid.

These are a few permutations within a vast and continuing stream of modern Medeas. (Further examples are discussed in the essay by Edith Hall in this Norton Critical Edition.) They testify to the ongoing effectiveness of the Medea myth for raising questions about marriage, parenthood, sexual jealousy, ethnicity, cross-cultural relations, and the status of women, and to the extraordinary stimulus to other writers offered by Euripides' play. They also return us to Euripides' own achievement in depicting a compelling heroine who remains so difficult to classify in familiar terms of foreign and native, male and female, divine and human.

The Staging of Euripides' Play

Euripides' *Medea* was first performed along with three other plays by Euripides (two other tragedies and a light-hearted, parodic satyr play) on a single day during the annual Festival of Dionysus. The venue was an open-air theater on the slopes of the Acropolis, the commanding hill at the center of Athens. The audience, which numbered around 10,000 people, most likely all men, sat on benches on the hillside, looking down at the performance space. This consisted of a flat circular area, the *orchestra* (or dance floor), where the chorus danced and sang; behind the *orchestra* there was a raised platform holding a simple building, the *skene*, which typically represented a house, like the house of Jason and Medea. The actors appeared on this platform, coming and going through a door in the *skene* or arriving at ground level by two paths on either side of that platform. Sometimes a much smaller platform, or *ekkyklema*, would be wheeled out through the door of the *skene* as a device for showing the inside of the house, especially the aftermath of some violent event which had taken place there. This is what the audience of *Medea* probably expected to see in the final scene. Instead, Medea appeared on top of the house, lifted up by a special crane, or *mechane*, that was more often used for the appearances of gods. The actors and chorus members were all men, dressed in costumes and wearing masks. Seen from a distance in this large outdoor setting, and without the ability to change their facial expressions, they had to rely on simple and stylized gestures to supplement their words.

The text that is translated here is a script of the words that were spoken, chanted, and sung at that performance.[5] All of the play was in verse, but part of what made tragedy an especially impressive and innovative form was the way it brought together different types of

---

5. I have based this translation on the edition in the Cambridge Greek and Latin Classics series by Donald Mastronarde, whose excellent commentary I have relied on throughout. I have also benefited from the edition and commentary for Aris & Philips by Judith Mossman.

performed poetry reflected in the different styles and types of line in this translation. The long speeches and dialogue were in iambic trimeter, the meter considered closest to everyday speech, and were simply spoken. Some passages, such as the entrance of the chorus and the more urgent utterances of Medea's Nurse, were in anapestic dimeter, a meter of shorter, more regular lines, each with a strong pause in the middle, sometimes chanted and sometimes spoken. The extended choral passages employed more intricate and variable meters and also involved both singing and dancing. The script indicates speakers but includes no stage directions; the action has to be deduced from the words of the text and is sometimes a matter of scholarly debate. We are missing the actors' costumes and gestures, the notes of the chorus' songs, and the steps of their dances. The text that remains offers us an opportunity to appreciate the verbal skill with which Euripides presents the strained relations and personal dilemmas of his characters and to imagine the full performance of which it forms only a part.

Acknowledgments

In preparing this Norton Critical Edition, I have benefited from many conversations with colleagues about the challenges and rewards of teaching *Medea*, and I particularly want to thank Ronnie Ancona and Caitlin Gillespie for showing me their syllabuses and telling me about their experiences. At Norton, I am grateful to Carol Bemis for her enthusiastic support of the project and to Rachel Goodman for her careful oversight and editorial advice. This translation was read, reread, and immensely improved by George Murnaghan Gordon and Emily Wilson. My first close encounters with the art of translation came through working with Stanley Lombardo on his versions of the Homeric epics. I have been consistently inspired by Stan's example, especially his exceptional ability to make characters in ancient texts sound like real human beings, and I am honored to dedicate this work to him.

The Text of
MEDEA

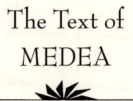

Medea

Cast of Characters

MEDEA
JASON
MEDEA'S NURSE
TUTOR OF MEDEA AND JASON'S SONS
CREON, KING OF CORINTH
AEGEUS, KING OF ATHENS
MESSENGER
CHORUS OF CORINTHIAN WOMEN
MEDEA AND JASON'S TWO SONS

Setting

Corinth, in front of the house in which MEDEA *and* JASON *have been living.*

[*Enter* MEDEA'S NURSE *from inside the house.*]
NURSE   If only the *Argo* had not slipped through
  the dark Clashing Rocks and landed at Colchis,
  if only that pine tree had not been cut down
  high on Mount Pelion and made into oars
  for the heroes who went out for the Golden Fleece,   5
  sent by King Pelias. Then my mistress Medea
  would never have sailed to the towers of Iolcus,
  overwhelmed by her love for Jason.
  She would not have talked the daughters of Pelias
  into killing their father, then fled here to Corinth   10
  with her husband and sons—where even in exile
  she has charmed the citizens of her new home,
  doing whatever she could to help out Jason.
  That is the strongest safeguard there is:
  when a wife always sides with her husband.   15
  But now they're at odds, their bond is infected.

3

Deserting his children along with my mistress,
Jason has climbed into a royal bed,
with the daughter of Creon, king of this land.
Poor Medea feels cruelly dishonored: 20
she keeps shouting about their oaths and bringing up
the solemn pledge of their joined right hands;
she keeps calling on the gods to witness
what kind of thanks she gets from Jason.
She stays in bed and won't eat; she hurts all over.   25
She's been weeping constantly since she heard
that she has been cast off by her husband.
She stares at the ground. When friends give advice,
she listens no more than a stone or the sea,
though sometimes she turns her pale neck away,   30
and sighs to herself about her dear father,
her homeland, her house—all those she betrayed
when she left with the man who now rejects her.
Poor thing, this disaster has made her learn
how hard it is to be cut off from home.   35
She hates her sons, gets no joy from seeing them.
I am afraid that she's planning something
[I know her: she's relentless and will not put up
with being mistreated. I can imagine
her sharpening a knife and stabbing someone,   40
sneaking into the house where the wedding bed's made,
to kill the king and his daughter's new bridegroom]¹
and will only cause herself more trouble.
She is fierce. If you get into a fight with her,
you won't come out singing a victory song.   45
          [*Enter the* TUTOR *with the two* BOYS.]
But here are the boys coming back from the track,
not thinking about their mother's problems—
young minds don't like to dwell on trouble.
TUTOR   Old servant of my mistress' house,
why do you stand here alone by the door,   50
pouring out your troubles to yourself?
Surely Medea doesn't want you to leave her?
NURSE   Old tutor of the sons of Jason,
when slaves are true-hearted, if their masters' luck
takes a turn for the worse, they suffer too.   55
I felt so wretched about my mistress
that I craved the relief of coming out here

---

1. Words in brackets here and throughout are considered by most scholars to be later
additions to the text, sometimes inserted by actors, sometimes by scholars and editors.

to tell her sad story to heaven and earth.
TUTOR   That poor woman has not stopped lamenting?
NURSE   If only! Her pain's still in its early stages.   60
TUTOR   What a fool, even if she is my mistress!
   She still doesn't know her latest troubles.
NURSE   What is it old man? Don't keep it to yourself.
TUTOR   No, nothing. I shouldn't have said what I did.
NURSE   Please don't leave a fellow slave in the dark.   65
   If it really matters, I won't tell anyone.
TUTOR   I heard someone talking, though he didn't notice.
   I was watching the old men playing checkers
   there where they sit by the spring of Peirene.
   He said that Creon, the king here in Corinth,   70
   is planning to exile these boys from the city,
   along with their mother. Whether this is true
   I have no idea. I certainly hope not.
NURSE   Would Jason really put his sons through that,
   even if he is on bad terms with their mother?   75
TUTOR   Old loyalties are trumped by new ones;
   and that man is no friend to this household.
NURSE   We're done for, if we face a new wave of troubles
   when we haven't bailed ourselves out from the last.
TUTOR   But now's not the right time for her to find out.   80
   So you should keep quiet. Don't say a word.
NURSE   Children, do you hear how your father treats you?
   He is my master: I can't curse him. But—
   it's clear he's willing to hurt his own family.
TUTOR   And who isn't? It should be plain to you   85
   that all people put themselves before others
   [sometimes with good reason, sometimes for gain]
   if this father prefers his new wife to his children.
NURSE   Go inside, boys. It will all be fine.
   Now you, make sure they are kept by themselves,   90
   not near their mother while she's so distraught.
   She looks at them the way a mad bull would,
   as if she's about to make some move.
   She won't stop raging until she crushes someone—
   better her enemies than people she loves.   95
      MEDEA [*from inside*]
   It's too much, too much to bear!
   I can't take any more. I want to die!
NURSE   Boys, see what I mean! Your mother
   keeps stirring up her angry heart.
   Quickly, quickly, into the house,   100
   but don't go near her: stay out of view.

Don't get too close, be on the watch
for her vengeful heart and her self-willed,
savage temper.
Go on inside, quick as you can.   105
Her grief is like a thundercloud
which her mounting fury will ignite.
And then what will she do,
this proud-to-the-core, uncurbable spirit
stung by sorrows?   110

       [*Exit the* TUTOR *and the* BOYS *into the house.*]

MEDEA   I'm abused, I'm abused, that's why I cry.
Boys, you are cursed, your mother is loathsome.
You might as well die along with your father.
Let the whole house come down!

NURSE   No, no! I don't like the sound of that.   115
Why blame your sons for their father's
offenses? Why turn on them?
Children, I'm sick with fear for you.
Our rulers have frightening tempers;
rarely governed, always in charge,   120
they can't let go of their anger.
Better to stay on a level plain.
I'd rather grow old in safety
and not lead a life of grandeur.
"Moderation" is a fine motto,   125
and we do well to live by it.
Reaching for more never brings
any real advantage in human life—
only greater ruin when an angry god
comes down on a house.   130

       [*Enter the* CHORUS OF CORINTHIAN WOMEN.]

CHORUS   I heard a voice! I heard the cry
of that poor Colchian woman!
Tell us old nurse, has she still not calmed down?
I'm sure I could hear through the double doors   134–35[2]
her wailing voice.
I get no joy from the grief in this house.
I consider myself a friend.

NURSE   There is no house. That's all gone.
The husband's possessed by a royal bed.   140
The wife wastes away in the innermost room,

---

2. In the Greek text, the lines of lyric passages are divided differently by different editors.
Groups of words conventionally numbered as separate lines may be combined in a single
line, as happens here and elsewhere in the edition used for this translation.

and will not be comforted
by anything a friend can say.
MEDEA   Let it come! A thunderbolt
straight through my head!   145
Why stay alive? In death
I can rest from a life I hate.
CHORUS   O Zeus, O Earth, O Light!
Do you hear the grief
in that girl's sad song?[3]   150
Why this foolish lust
for a fatal resting place?
You want death to hurry up?
Do not ever ask for that.
So your husband adores someone else.   155
You should not rage at him.
Zeus will stand up for you.
Do not ruin yourself mourning that man.   158–59
MEDEA   Mighty Themis! Holy Artemis![4]   160
Do you see what I suffer—even after
I bound my hateful husband with solemn oaths?
I'd gladly watch him and his new bride
being smashed to pieces with their whole house
for the huge wrong they have done to me.   165
My father! My city!—shamefully lost
when I killed my brother.
NURSE   You can hear what gods she calls on:
unfailing Themis and great Zeus,
who oversees the oaths of mortals.   170
There is no way she'll end her anger
with just some empty gesture.
CHORUS   If she would meet us
face-to-face
and listen to our words,   175
she might let go of the rage in her heart,
and soften her harsh temper.
I am always eager
to help a friend.
Go bring her out of the house.   180
Tell her we're on her side.
You have to act before she can hurt
those boys in there: grief spurs her on.

---

3. In the original Greek, the chorus refers to Medea with the word for a bride or new wife, accentuating her unsettled situation.
4. Virgin goddess associated with women's transition to marriage. *Themis*: venerable goddess associated with justice and proper order.

NURSE   I doubt I can persuade her,
   but I'll do as you ask me to,   185
   and make one last attempt.
   When we try to speak to her,
   she glares at us like a bull
   or a lioness with newborn cubs.
   I have to say our ancestors   190
   showed very little sense
   when they invented melodies
   for revels, festivals, and feasts,
   the sweetest sounds in life,
   but made no songs or harmonies   195
   to soothe the bitter grief
   that leads to death and devastation
   and brings whole houses down.
   A musical cure for that would be
   worth having. Why should people sing   200
   when they're gathered at a feast
   and there's joy enough already
   in the meal's abundance?
                     [*Exit the* NURSE *into the house.*]
CHORUS   I hear the pain in her loud laments;
   she shouts out high and shrill,   205
   at the faithless husband who spurns her bed.
   She calls on Themis to hear her wrongs,
   daughter of Zeus, upholder of oaths.   208–09
   Because of an oath, she crossed to Greece,   210
   sailing on the dark night waves   211–12
   of the Black Sea's watery gate.
                 [*Enter* MEDEA *from the house, with attendants.*]
MEDEA   Women of Corinth, I have left the house
   to avoid offending you. With many people,   215
   you know that they're proud whether they stay home
   or go out. But others are seen as aloof
   just because they choose to lead quiet lives.
   People aren't fair when they judge with their eyes.
   Not taking the trouble to look inside,   220
   they hate someone on sight who's done them no harm.
   So a stranger really has to fit in.
   It's not good when even a self-willed native
   is out of touch and rude to fellow citizens.
   In my case, this unexpected calamity   225
   has crushed my spirit. I am finished, friends,
   done with life's joys. I wish I was dead.
   My husband, who was everything to me,

is actually, I now see, the worst of men.
Of all living, breathing, thinking creatures   230
women are the most absolutely wretched.
First, you have to pay an enormous sum
to buy a husband who, to make things worse,
gets to be the master of your body.5
And it's a gamble: you're as likely to get   235
a bad one as a good one. Divorce means disgrace
for women, and you can't say no to a husband.
Finding herself among strange laws and customs,
a wife needs to be clairvoyant; she has not
learned at home how to deal with her mate.   240
If we work hard at all these things,
and our husbands don't chafe at the yoke,
that's an enviable life. If not, we're better off dead.
A man who feels oppressed by the company at home,
goes out and gets relief for his low spirits   245
[turning to a friend or someone else his age],
but we can only look to that one other person.
They tell us that we enjoy a sheltered life,
staying at home while they are out fighting.
How wrong they are! I would rather face battle   250
three times than go through childbirth once.
But it isn't the same for you as for me.
This is your city. The houses you grew up in,
all your daily pleasures, your friends, are here.
I am alone, without a city, disowned   255
by my husband, snatched from a foreign land.
I have no mother, brother, or other family
to shelter me now that disaster has struck.
So I have just one thing to ask of you:
if some plan or scheme occurs to me   260
by which I can get back at my husband
[and the king and his daughter, Jason's new wife],
say nothing. A woman is usually quite timid,
shying away from battles and weapons,
but if her marriage bed's dishonored,   265
no one has a deadlier heart.
CHORUS   I will do that. You are right to pay him back,
     Medea. I can see why you're aggrieved.
          [*Enter* CREON.]
But here is Creon, ruler of this land,
coming to announce some new decision.   270

---

5. A bride's family paid a dowry to the groom upon her marriage.

CREON You, with your scowls and your spite for your husband,
    Medea, I command you to leave this land.
    Take your two sons and go into exile—
    and no delaying. I have authority
    over this decree, and I'm not going home   275
    until I've placed you outside our borders.
MEDEA Oh no! I am completely destroyed.
    My enemies are spreading their sails to the wind,
    and I can't disembark from disaster.
    But bad as things are, I have to ask: 280
    what's your reason, Creon, for throwing me out?
CREON I'll come right out and say it: I'm afraid
    that you'll do my daughter some incurable harm.
    There are many signs that point to this.
    You are clever and skilled at causing damage,   285
    and you feel injured in your empty bed.
    People have told me you're threatening us all:
    the bride's father, the bridegroom, and the bride.
    So I'm acting first to protect myself.
    I would rather earn your hatred now   290
    than regret later on that I was too lenient.
MEDEA Not again!
    Creon, the same thing keeps happening:
    my reputation gets me into trouble.
    No man who has his wits about him
    would raise his sons to be too clever.   295
    Not only will they be considered lazy,
    they'll be resented by their fellow citizens.
    When you propose a clever plan to dullards,
    they see you as useless rather than clever;
    and those who are thought to be sophisticated   300
    are bothered when the people think you're smarter.
    This is exactly what has happened to me.
    I'm clever, so I'm envied by one group
    [to some I'm idle, to some the reverse]
    and annoy the rest—cleverness has limits.   305
    I know you're afraid I'll do you some harm.
    But why be worried? I am in no position
    to go on the offensive against a king.
    How have you wronged me? You gave your daughter
    to the man you wanted to. The one I hate   310
    is my husband. You were acting sensibly.
    I don't blame you because you're doing well.
    Marry her off! Best of luck to all! But—
    just let me stay. I may have been mistreated,

but I'll keep quiet, yielding to my betters.   315
CREON Your words sound pleasing, but I am afraid
    that you have some evil plan in your heart.
    In fact, I trust you less than I did before.
    A hot-tempered woman—or man—is easier
    to guard against than a silent, clever one.   320
    No, you have to leave at once. Enough talking.
    It is decided: you are my enemy,
    and none of your tricks can keep you here.
       [MEDEA *kneels and grasps Creon's knees
       and hand in a gesture of ritual supplication.*]
MEDEA No! By your knees! By your daughter the bride!
CREON Your words are wasted. You will never convince me.   325
MEDEA You're ignoring my prayers and driving me out?
CREON I care about my family, not about you.
MEDEA My lost home! I can't stop thinking about it.
CREON That's what means most to me, after my children.
MEDEA Oh, what a disaster to fall in love!   330
CREON That depends, I'd say, on the circumstances.
MEDEA Zeus, be sure to notice who's making me suffer.
CREON Don't be a fool! Go, and take my troubles with you.
MEDEA I have troubles too, far more than I need.
CREON My guards are preparing to throw you out.   335
MEDEA No, not that! Creon, I implore you.
CREON So you're determined to make this difficult.
MEDEA I will leave. I don't ask you to change that.
CREON Then why keep pressing me? Let go of my hand.
MEDEA Just let me stay here for one more day   340
    so I can work out my plans for exile
    and make some arrangements for my sons,
    since their father is not inclined to help.
    Show them some pity. You have children yourself;
    it's only natural to wish these boys well.   345
    I'm not worried about exile for myself
    but I feel the hardship it brings my sons.
CREON I'm really not a tyrant at heart:
    to my own cost, I have listened to others.
    Even though I know it's not a good idea,   350
    you get your wish. But I warn you,
    if tomorrow's sun finds you and your boys
    still inside the borders of this country,
    you will die. I say it, and I mean it.
    So stay on, if you must, for this one day;   355
    you won't have time to do the harm I fear.
              [*Exit* CREON. MEDEA *stands up.*]

CHORUS   Poor, poor woman,
    weighed down by troubles,
    where can you turn? What welcome,
    what house, what sheltering land   360
    [will you find]?
    Medea, some god has tossed you
    into a sea of constant trials.
MEDEA   It's bad all around. Who would deny that?
    But don't imagine that everything's settled.   365
    There are struggles ahead for the bridal pair,
    and many ordeals for the bride's father.
    Would I have fawned on him like that
    without something to gain or a secret plan?
    There wouldn't have been that talking and touching. 370
    But he is such a credulous fool:
    when he had a chance to throw me out
    and foil my plans, he gave me one more day
    to make corpses out of my three tormenters—
    the father, the daughter, and my own husband.   375
    I can think of many routes to their death;
    I'm not sure, friends, which one to try first,
    whether to set the newlyweds' house on fire,
    or stab someone's liver with a sharpened sword,
    silently entering the bridal bedroom.   380
    But there is a risk: if I am caught
    sneaking into the house, I will lose my life
    and give my enemies a chance to laugh.
    The safest course is the one I know best:
    to poison them with deadly drugs.   385
    That's it then.
    But once they are dead—then what city
    will take me in? Where is the friend
    who will save my life by giving me shelter?
    Nowhere. So I will wait a little while,
    and if some tower of safety appears   390
    I will kill them with a hidden trick.
    But if I am forced to act in the open,
    I will strike with a sword. Ready to die,
    I will go to the very edge of daring.
    By Hecate,[6] whom I most revere,   395
    the goddess who is my chosen ally,
    who haunts the darkest corners of my house,
    they will not get away with causing this pain.

6. Goddess associated with magic and witchcraft.

I will make sure they find their marriage bitter,
and bitter the tie with Creon, bitter my exile.   400
Now Medea, use everything you know;
you must plot and scheme as you approach
the dreadful act that will test your spirit.
Do you see what is being done to you?
Do not be mocked by this Sisyphean wedding;[7]   405
You spring from a noble father and Helios the sun.
You have the skill, and along with that
a woman's nature—useless for doing good
but just right for contriving evil.

CHORUS   Sacred streams are flowing backwards;   410–11
    right and wrong are turned around.
    It's men who do the shady scheming,
    swear by the gods, then break their oaths.
    News of this will bring us glory,   415–16
    rightful honor for the female race;   417–18
    women will at last be free
    from the taint of ugly rumors.   420

Enough of ancient poets' legends
that tell of us as breaking faith!
The lord of song, divine Apollo,
did not grant the lyre's sweet music
for the speaking of our minds,   425
or I could have made an answer   426–27
to the stories spread by men.   428–29
Time's long record speaks on both sides.   430–31

Mad with love, you left your father.
Sailing through the briny border
of the double Clashing Rocks,
you settled in a land of strangers.   435
Now your husband's left your bed;
so you're banished from this country,
a lonely exile without rights.

All over Greece, oaths prove hollow;
shame has melted into air.   440
And for you there's no safe harbor
in your lost paternal home,
no escaping from your troubles,

---

7. In the spirit of Sisyphus, a legendary Corinthian trickster, eventually punished in Hades
with the eternal task of pushing a rock uphill only to have it roll down again.

as you watch a royal princess
take your marriage and your house. 445

[*Enter* JASON.]

JASON This is not the first time that I've observed
how impossible a stubborn person can be.
You had the chance to stay in this country,
going along with what your betters had planned,
but you're being thrown out for your pointless rants, 450
and there's nothing I can do. Fine! Don't stop
talking about "that disgusting Jason."
But for what you've said about the rulers—
you are lucky that it's only exile.
The king gets more and more angry. I've tried 455
to calm him down, hoping you could stay.
Yet you keep up this nonsense, raving on
against the king. So you're being thrown out.
Still, I am not one to abandon family.
I'm here now to look out for your interests, 460
so you and the boys don't leave without money
or other provisions. Exile's not easy.
Maybe you can't stop hating me,
but I'll always want what is best for you.

MEDEA You really are disgusting! That sums up 465
what I have to say about your spinelessness.
You've really come here, when you are hated
[by me and the gods and everyone else]?
It's not some daring noble endeavor
to look friends in the face after you've wronged them, 470
but the lowest and sickest of human failings:
shamelessness. Still it is good that you came.
If I name all your appalling actions,
I'll get some relief, and you'll feel much worse.
Let me start at the very beginning: 475
I saved you, as every Greek knows
who shipped out with you on the *Argo*,
when you had to bring the fire-breathing bulls
under a yoke and sow a deadly field.
And that serpent, which never slept 480
and held the Golden Fleece in winding coils,
I killed it, bringing you the light of salvation.
And as for me, I cheated my father
and followed you to Iolcus and Mount Pelion,
infatuated, not thinking straight. 485
I made Pelias die in the most gruesome way,

at his daughters' hands; I ruined his house.
All of this I did for you, you lowlife,
and you have deserted me for someone new
even though we have children. If we didn't,   490
you could be forgiven for wanting her.
Our oaths mean nothing to you. I can't tell
if you think those gods have lost their power,
or imagine that the rules have changed for mortals—
since you're well aware that you broke a promise.   495
My right hand here—to think I let you touch it,
and to clasp my knees. I was abused
by a swindler, deceived by false hopes.
Still, let me ask you for some friendly advice.
(But why should I think you'd help me now?   500
Well, if I ask you, it'll make you look worse.)
So where should I go? To my father's house
which I betrayed when I ran off with you?
To the poor daughters of Pelias? I'm sure
I'd be welcome there, where I killed their father.   505
That is how it stands: my friends at home
hate me now, and those I should have treated well
I turned into enemies by helping you.
For what I did, you made me the envy
of all Greek women—with such a marvelous catch,   510
such a loyal husband that I'm being expelled,
a miserable outcast from this country,
without any friends, alone with my sons.
It doesn't look so good for the bridegroom—
children out begging with the woman who saved him.   515
Zeus, you should have given us a touchstone
for human nature as you did for gold!
We need a way to tell from someone's looks
whether or not he's base on the inside.
CHORUS   There is a dreadful, incurable anger   520
    when former lovers fall to fighting.
JASON   It seems I'll have to be a skillful speaker,
    and, like a careful pilot, reef in my sails
    if I have any hope of outrunning
    the surging onslaught of your angry words.   525
    You make much of the help you gave me,
    but I say that it was Aphrodite⁸ alone
    who assured the success of my venture.
    You may be quick-witted, but like it or not,

---

8. Goddess of love; her son Eros made people fall in love by shooting them with his arrows.

I could tell how you were compelled   530
by Eros' sure arrows to save my life.
But no need to tally this up exactly:
whatever you did was helpful enough.
Still, it's my view that you got much more
out of my being saved than I ever did.   535
First of all, you are living in Greece,
not some foreign country. Here you find justice
and the rule of law; force has no standing.
And all of Greece knows how clever you are;
you're famous. If you lived at the ends of the earth,   540
no one would ever have heard of you.
I see no point in a house full of gold,
or a gift for singing better than Orpheus,[9]
without the good fortune of being well known.
So—since you have turned this into a contest,   545
those are the things I accomplished for you.
Now, on this royal marriage that you dislike,
I can show you that I acted wisely,
soberly, and in the best interest
of you and the boys. Just stay calm for a moment.   550
When I moved here from the city of Iolcus,
I was dragged down by impossible problems.
What better solution could there be
for an exile like me than to marry the princess?
You are upset, but it's not what you think,   555
that I'm sick of you and smitten with this girl,
or want some prize for having lots of children;
I am satisfied with the ones we've got.
It's so we'll live well and won't be in need.
And that is important. I can tell you: 560
everyone steers clear of a penniless friend.
I will raise our sons as befits our family
and add some brothers to the boys you gave me.
Bringing them together in a single tribe,
I'll prosper. What are more children to you?   565
In my case, having new offspring benefits
the older ones. Is that such a bad plan?
You wouldn't say so if it weren't for the sex.
You women reach the point where you think
if all's well in the bedroom everything's fine;   570
but if some trouble arises there,
you insist on rejecting whatever's best.

9. Legendary singer who could set animals, trees, and stones in motion; one of the Argonauts.

We should have some other way of getting children.
Then there would be no female race,
and mankind would be free from trouble.   575
CHORUS   Jason, you've put together a polished speech.
But, at the risk of disagreeing, I say
that you do wrong to desert your wife.
MEDEA   I'm clearly different from everyone else.
To me, a scoundrel who is good at speaking   580
should have to pay a special price for that.
Since he knows he can gloss over his crimes,
he'll try anything, though cleverness has limits.
That's what you are. So don't try to impress me
with clever words. A single point refutes you: 585
if you were so noble, you would have gotten
my consent to this marriage, not kept it secret.
JASON   Oh yes, I'm sure you would have agreed
if I had told you then, when even now
you can't help reacting with fury.   590
MEDEA   That wasn't it. You thought a foreign wife
would be an embarrassment in years to come.
JASON   You need to understand. It is not for the woman
that I'm taking on this royal marriage.
It's what I told you before. I only want   595
to give you protection and safeguard our children
by fathering royal siblings for them.
MEDEA   Spare me a life of shameful wealth
or a good situation that eats at my soul.
JASON   You know what you really need to pray for?   600
The sense not to see a good thing as shameful,
not to think you're suffering when you're doing fine.
MEDEA   Go on, be cruel. You have a safe home here,
while I'll be cast out with nowhere to go.
JASON   You chose that. Don't blame anyone else.   605
MEDEA   How? I betrayed you by marrying somebody?
JASON   By rudely cursing the royal family.
MEDEA   Well, I'll bring a curse to your house too.
JASON   I have had enough of squabbling with you,
but if you want some money from me   610
to provide for you and the boys in exile,
just say so. I want to be generous
and can contact friends who will treat you well.
You would be an idiot to turn me down.
You'll be better off if you forget your anger.   615
MEDEA   I want nothing to do with your friends.
I won't take anything you give. Don't bother.

No good comes from a bad man's gifts.
JASON   Well, the gods will witness how eager I am
to do what I can for you and the boys.   620
You are so stubborn that you reject what's good
and snub your friends. You will suffer all the more.
MEDEA   Just go! I'm sure that staying away this long
has left you longing for your new bride.
Go play the groom. And maybe I'm right to hope   625
you will have a marriage that makes you weep.

                                                  [*Exit* JASON.]

CHORUS   Overwhelming love never leads to virtue,   627–28
             or a good reputation.   629–30
Just enough Aphrodite is the greatest blessing.   631–32
Goddess, don't aim at me with your golden bow   633–34
             and arrows dipped in desire.   635

I choose to be wooed by sober restraint,
             best gift of the gods.
I won't have Aphrodite stirring up quarrels,   638–39
by making me fall for a stranger. She should grant us   640–42
             harmonious marriages.   643–44

Beloved country! Beloved home!   645
May I never lose my city;
that is a life without hope,   647–48
the hardest of trials to bear.
Better, far better to die,   650
than ever come to that.
There is no deeper pain
than being cut off from home.

I have seen it for myself;
no one had to tell me.   655
For you have no city,
no friends who feel for you
in your bitter struggles.
Whoever doesn't honor friends
with an open heart,   660
deserves an awful death
and is no friend of mine.

       [*Enter* AEGEUS.]
AEGEUS   Hello, Medea! And all good wishes—
the warmest of greetings among true friends.

MEDEA	Good wishes to you, son of wise Pandion,	665
	Aegeus! Where are you coming from?	
AEGEUS	Straight from Apollo's ancient oracle.	
MEDEA	What took you there, to the center of the earth?	
AEGEUS	I wanted to know how I might have children.	
MEDEA	Goodness! Have you been childless all this time?	670
AEGEUS	Yes, childless—thanks, I am sure, to some god.	
MEDEA	Do you have a wife, or do you sleep alone?	
AEGEUS	I'm married; I have a wife who shares my bed.	
MEDEA	And what did Apollo say about children?	
AEGEUS	Subtler words than a man can make sense of.	675
MEDEA	Am I allowed to know what he said?	
AEGEUS	Of course. I need the help of your clever mind.	
MEDEA	Then if it's allowed, tell me what he said.	
AEGEUS	Not to untie the foot of the wineskin . . . [1]	
MEDEA	Before doing what? Or arriving where?	680
AEGEUS	Before I get back to my ancestral hearth.	
MEDEA	And what's your reason for landing here?	
AEGEUS	There's a man called Pittheus, king of Troezen.	
MEDEA	Son of Pelops, said to be very pious.	
AEGEUS	I want to ask him about the prophecy.	685
MEDEA	Yes, he's wise and knows about such things.	
AEGEUS	And he's my most trusted comrade at war.	
MEDEA	Well good luck! I hope you get what you want.	
AEGEUS	But why are you looking so red-eyed and pale?	
MEDEA	It turns out I have the worst possible husband.	690
AEGEUS	What are you saying? Tell me what's upset you.	
MEDEA	Jason mistreats me though I've given him no cause.	
AEGEUS	What is he doing? Explain what you mean.	
MEDEA	He put another woman in charge of our house.	
AEGEUS	Would he do something so improper?	695
MEDEA	He would. So I, once prized, am now dismissed.	
AEGEUS	Is he in love? Or has he fallen out with you?	
MEDEA	So much in love that he's abandoned his family.	
AEGEUS	Well, if he's that bad, forget about him.	
MEDEA	He's in love with the thought of a royal match.	700
AEGEUS	Then tell me: who is the new wife's father?	
MEDEA	Creon, who rules right here in Corinth.	
AEGEUS	Well, I can see why you are angry.	
MEDEA	Devastated. And I'm being expelled.	
AEGEUS	From bad to worse! What's the reason for that?	705
MEDEA	Creon has declared me an exile from Corinth.	

---

1. Leather container for wine in the shape of an animal, with a "foot" that served as an opening.

AEGEUS   And Jason accepts this? That's not right.
MEDEA   He protests now, but he'll gladly put up with it.
    So I'm reaching out my hands to your face
    and making myself your suppliant.   710
    Take pity on me in my wretched state,
    don't let me become a lonely outcast.
    Take me into your country and your house.
    Do this, and may the gods grant your wish.
    May you live out the happy life you long for.   715
    You don't know how lucky you are to find me:
    I can take care of your lack of children.
    I know the right drugs to make you a father.
AEGEUS   There are many reasons why I want to help.
    First the gods, who favor suppliants,   720
    and then the children you say I could have—
    something where I'm really at a loss.
    So, if you can get yourself to my land,
    I will try to give you proper shelter.
    [I should make one thing plain to you: 725
    I'm not willing to take you away from here.]
    If you leave this place on your own
    and arrive at my house, also on your own,
    you will be safe. I will not hand you over.
    But I can't offend my friends while I'm here.   730
MEDEA   Agreed. Now if you could make a formal pledge,
    then I will feel you've treated me perfectly.
AEGEUS   You don't trust me? What's on your mind?
MEDEA   I trust you. But Pelias's family hates me,
    and Creon too. If you are bound by oaths,   735
    you can't let them take me from your land.
    If you just say yes and don't swear by the gods,
    you might end up being gracious and giving in
    to their demands. I'm completely powerless,
    while they have wealth and status on their side.   740
AEGEUS   You clearly have this all figured out.
    So if you think I should, I won't refuse.
    This will put me in a stronger position,
    with a good excuse to give your enemies,
    and it helps you. Name the gods I should swear by.   745
MEDEA   Swear by the Earth and by the Sun, father
    of my father, and the entire race of gods.
AEGEUS   To do—or not to do—what? Say it.
MEDEA   Not ever to cast me out from your land,
    and if some enemy tries to lead me away,   750
    not to allow it while you live and breathe.

AEGEUS   I swear by the Earth and the light of the Sun,
   and all the gods, I will do as you say.
MEDEA   Good. And the penalty if you break the oath?
AEGEUS   Whatever ungodly people have to suffer.   755
MEDEA   A good journey to you. All is in place.
   I will come to your city as soon as I can,
   once I have fulfilled my plans and desires.
CHORUS   May Hermes, guide of travelers,
   speed you to your home,   760
   and may you gain your heart's desire,
   for you are an honorable man, Aegeus,
   that is clear to me.

                                            [*Exit* AEGEUS.]

MEDEA   O Zeus, O Justice born of Zeus, O Sun!
   Now, friends, I know I am on the path   765
   to glorious victory over my enemies.
   Now I feel sure they will have to pay.
   I was at a loss, and then this man appeared,
   who will be a safe haven when my plots are done.
   I can fasten my mooring line to him   770
   when I have made my way to Athens.
   And now I will tell you what I have in mind;
   listen to this, though I doubt you will like it.
   I will send a trusted servant to Jason
   who will ask him to meet me face-to-face.   775
   When he comes, I will give a soothing speech
   about how I agree with him and now believe
   that his faithless marriage is a first-rate plan,
   advantageous and well thought through.
   Then I'll plead for the children to stay behind;   780
   not that I want to leave them in this hostile land
   [and have my children mistreated by enemies];
   it's part of a trick to kill the king's daughter.
   I'll send them to her with gifts in their hands
   [for the bride, so they won't have to leave],   785
   a delicate robe and a golden crown.
   Once she takes this finery and puts it on,
   she—and whoever touches her—will die
   because of poisons I will spread on the gifts.
   That's all there is to say on that subject.   790
   But the thought of what I have to do next
   fills me with grief: I need to kill the children,
   no one should hope to spare them that.
   Once I've torn Jason's house apart, I'll leave
   and pay no price for the poor boys' death.   795

I will bring myself to this unholy act
because I cannot let my enemies laugh.
[So be it! Why should I live? I have no country,
no home, no way of escaping my troubles.]
It was a bad mistake to leave my home   800
swayed by the words of a man from Greece,
but with the gods' help I will punish him.
He won't see the children we had grow up
and he won't be able to have any more
with his brand-new bride: no, she's doomed   805
to an agonizing death from my drugs.
No one should think I am meek and mild
or passive. I am quite the opposite:
harsh to enemies and loyal to friends,
the kind of person whose life has glory.   810
CHORUS   Now that you have shared this plan with me,
    I want to help you and to honor human law,
    and so I say to you: don't do this thing.
MEDEA   I see why you say that, but there's no other way;
    you haven't been through the troubles I have.   815
CHORUS   You would be able to kill your own children?
MEDEA   It is the surest way to wound my husband.
CHORUS   And to make yourself impossibly wretched.
MEDEA   So be it. We have done enough talking.
        [MEDEA turns to her attendants.]
    One of you servants, go bring Jason here.
    And you, the friends I trust with my closest secrets,   820
    if you respect me and have women's hearts,
    you will say nothing about my plan.
                        [Exit one of Medea's attendants.]

CHORUS   The sons of Erectheus,[2] long blessed
        with wealth,
    Athenian offspring of the Olympian gods,
    raised in a land untouched by war,   825
    nourished by the glorious arts,   826–27
    stride easily through the radiant air,   828–29
    where once, it's said, the holy Muses   830–31
    gave birth to golden Harmony.   832–33

    I've heard that Aphrodite dips her cup   835
    in the streams of clear Cephisus,[3]

2. Legendary early king of Athens.
3. River running through Athens.

and sends sweet breezes through the land.   837–38
Crowned with a twining garland   839–40
of fragrant, blooming roses,   841–42
she sets Desire at Wisdom's side   843–44
to foster all that's good.   845

How can that land of sacred streams,
that open-hearted city,
be a fitting home for you,
unholy woman,
killer of children?   850
Think what it is to strike a child!
Think who you are killing!
By every sacred thing
I beg of you:
spare those boys.   855

How can you find the will,
how can you steel your mind,
to lift your hand against your sons,
to do this awful thing?
How will you stop your tears,   860
when you see them dying?
They will huddle at your knees,
and you will not be able
to spill their blood
with a steady heart.   865

    [*Enter* JASON.]
JASON   You called me, so I've come. You may hate me,
    but I won't let you down. I'm eager to hear
    what you think you may need from me after all.
MEDEA   Jason, please overlook what I said before.
    You should be willing to put up with my fits,   870
    for the sake of the love that we once shared.
    And I have been thinking all of this over
    and berating myself for being obtuse.
    Why turn on those who wish me well,
    picking a fight with the country's rulers   875
    and my husband, who serves us all
    by marrying a princess and giving our sons
    new royal brothers? Why be angry?
    The gods will provide, so how can I lose?
    Shouldn't I think of the boys? I can't forget   880
    that I'm an exile and have no friends.

When I look at it that way, I can see
I've been confused and my rage was pointless.
I'm all for it now. I think you are wise
to arrange this connection. I'm the fool: 885
I should have thrown myself into these plans
and helped them along, tending the bed
and gladly serving your new bride.
It's just that women are . . . well, not quite wicked,
but anyway you shouldn't copy us   890
and get caught up in silly quarrels.
Please forgive me: I was wrong before
and now I understand much better.
Boys, boys! Come out of the house
to greet your father and talk to him.   895

[*Enter the* TUTOR *and the* TWO BOYS *from the house.*]

End your anger towards one you should love
just as I, your mother, am doing.
We have made our peace, there is no more strife.
So take his hand. But oh, when I think
of all the trouble the future conceals!   900
My children, in your lives to come,
will you reach out a loving arm to me?
I am so quick to weep and full of fear.
I'm making up my quarrel with your father
but even so my eyes are filled with tears.   905

CHORUS   Tears are coming to my eyes as well.
I only hope there's nothing worse ahead.

JASON   I'm pleased with your present behavior, Medea,
and I forgive the past: of course a woman minds
if her husband decides to import a new wife.   910
But now your feelings have turned around,
and you recognize the better course at last.
That shows you are a sensible woman.
Now boys, don't think I've been a negligent father.
With the gods' help, I've secured your position.   915
I am quite sure that you will be leaders
here in Corinth, you and your new siblings.
Just be strong and stay well. I will do the rest,
along with whatever god's on our side.
I hope to see you turning into fine young men,   920
and towering over my enemies.
But you, why are your cheeks covered with tears?
Why do you look pale and turn away?
Aren't you happy with what I am saying?

MEDEA   It's nothing—just the thought of these children.   925

JASON   Don't worry. I will take care of everything.

MEDEA   You're right. I can rely on your promises.
   It's just that women are made for tears.

JASON   But why are you so sad about the children?

MEDEA   I am their mother. And your hopes for their future   930
   filled me with fear that those things won't happen.
   Now some of what you are here to discuss
   has been settled, so I'll move on to the rest:
   since the rulers have decided to banish me
   (and I really do see that it's for the best   935
   so I won't be in your way, or theirs,
   since I can't help seeming antagonistic),
   I will comply and leave the country.
   But the boys should stay here and be raised by you;
   ask Creon to spare them this exile.   940

JASON   I may not convince him, but I will try.

MEDEA   You should get your bride to ask her father
   to let the boys stay here in this country.

JASON   Good idea. She'll do it if I ask her:
   she is a woman like any other.   945

MEDEA   And I will be part of this effort too.
   I will send her the most splendid gifts
   that can be found anywhere in the world
   [a delicate robe and a golden crown]
   and the boys will take them. Now servants,   950
   bring out the presents right away.

                   [Exit an attendant into the house.]

   She will have many reasons to rejoice:
   In you she has the best of husbands
   and she will wear the ornaments
   that my grandfather Helios left to his heirs.   955

      [Enter the attendant with the gifts.]

   Take these wedding presents, boys,
   carry them to the happy royal bride.
   They will be perfect gifts for her.

JASON   That's ridiculous! Don't deprive yourself.
   Do you think the royal house needs dresses,   960
   or gold? You should hold on to these things.
   I am sure that her high regard for me
   will matter more than material objects.

MEDEA   No. They say even the gods are moved by gifts.
   For us, gold counts more than a million words.   965
   Her fortunes are high, she has a god on her side,
   she's young and has power. I'd give my life,
   and not just gold, to save the boys from exile.

My sons, go into that fine rich house;
appeal to your father's new wife, my mistress;   970
ask for reprieve from a life of exile,
and hand her the gifts. It is essential
that she herself takes them from you.
Hurry! And bring back the good news
that you have made your mother's wish come true.   975

        [*Exit* JASON, *the* BOYS, *and the* TUTOR.]

CHORUS   No more hoping that those children will live.
No more, for they are on the road to murder.
The bride will reach out for the golden chains,
poor thing, she'll reach out for her doom.
With her own hands she will place in her hair   980–81
the finery of Death.

Lured by their lovely unearthly glow
she'll put on the dress and the wrought-gold crown
and make her marriage in the world below.   985
That is the trap into which she will fall,
poor thing, she will follow her destiny,   987–88
inescapable Death.

And you, unlucky groom,   990
new member of the royal house,
you are not able to see
that you're leading your boys to their life's end,
and bringing a hateful death to your bride.
You have no idea of your fate.   995

And you, poor mother of these boys,
I also grieve for you,
since you are set on making them die
because of the bed which your husband left.
He thoughtlessly abandoned you   1000
and lives with another wife.

        [*Enter the* BOYS *and the* TUTOR.]

TUTOR   Mistress! The boys are spared the fate of exile!
The princess gladly accepted the gifts
with her own hands. She is on their side.
But . . .
why are you upset at this good fortune?   1005
[Why have you turned your face away?
Why aren't you happy with what I'm saying?]

MEDEA Oh no!

TUTOR That doesn't fit with the news I brought.

MEDEA Oh no, oh no!

TUTOR What is it that I don't understand?

Was I wrong to think I was bringing good news?   1010

MEDEA You bring the news you bring. It's not your fault.

TUTOR But why are you crying and turning away?

MEDEA I can't help it, old friend. Terrible plans
have been devised by the gods—and by me.

TUTOR The boys' good standing here will bring you back.   1015

MEDEA First I, in my grief, will bring others down.

TUTOR Other mothers have been torn from their children.
You are mortal and must accept misfortune.

MEDEA Yes, yes, I will. Now you go inside.
Take care of whatever the boys might need.   1020

[*Exit the* TUTOR *into the house.*]

O boys, boys, you still have a city,
and a home where, leaving me for good,
you will be cut off from your unhappy mother.
I will be an exile in a foreign land
without the delight of watching you thrive,   1025
without the joy of preparing your weddings,
tending the bath and the bed, lifting the torches.
How much my own strong will has cost me!
I get nothing, boys, from raising you,
from running myself ragged with endless work.   1030
The birth pangs I endured were pointless.
It pains me to think what hopes I had
that you would care for me in old age
and prepare me for burial when I die—
the thing that everyone wants. But now   1035
that happy dream is dead. Deprived of you,
I will live out my life in bitter grief.
And you will embark on a different life
with no more loving eyes for your mother.
But why, why, boys, are you looking at me?   1040
Why do you smile for this one last time?
Oh, what should I do? I lost heart, my friends,
as soon as I saw their beaming faces.
I can't do it. So much for my plans!
I will take the boys away from here.   1045
Why make them suffer to hurt their father
if it means I suffer twice as much myself?
I can't do that. So much for my plans!
But wait! Can I really bear to be laughed at

and let my enemies go unpunished?   1050
I have to steel myself. I can't be weak
and let those tender thoughts take over.
Children, into the house. And anyone
who is out of place at my sacrifice
can stay away. I will not spare my hand.   1055
But oh . . .
My angry heart, do not go through with this.
For all your pain, let the children live.
They can be with you and bring you joy.
And yet—by the vengeful spirits of deepest Hades—
there is no way I can allow my enemies   1060
to seize my children and to mistreat them.
[It is certain that they have to die. And so
I should kill them, since I gave them life.]
It is all in place: she cannot escape;
the crown is on her head; the royal bride   1065
revels in her new dress. I heard it clearly.
Having set out myself on the darkest road
I will send my sons down one that's even darker.
I will talk to them. Give me, my children,
give me, your mother, your hands to kiss.   1070
Oh this hand! this mouth! this face!
Oh my dear ones, my noble sons!
Be happy—but there. Your father wrecked
what we had here. Oh the joy of holding them,
of their tender skin, of their sweet breath.   1075
Go in! Go in! I can no longer bear
to look at you. My grief is too strong.
I see the horror of what I am doing,
but anger overwhelms my second thoughts—[4]
anger, boundless source of evil.   1080

[*Exit the* BOYS *into the house.*]

CHORUS   I have often entered into
complicated trains of thought,
and pursued much deeper questions
than women are supposed to tackle.
For there's a Muse that favors me   1085
and confers the gift of wisdom,
not on all, but on a few—

4. The proper translation of this line is a matter of debate, since the same Greek word is used for "second thoughts" as for the plans they would rule out. An alternative way of interpreting the line is "Anger is the force that drives my plans."

[you'll find some women here and there]
who are not strangers to that Muse.
So I can say that those who never   1090
find themselves producing children
are more fortunate by far
than those who do.
The childless never need to ask
whether children are in the end,   1095
a curse or blessing in human life;
and since they have none of their own,
they are spared a world of trouble.
Those parents who are blessed
with houses full of growing children
are constantly worn out by worry: 1100
will they be able to raise them well
and leave behind enough to live on?
And all along it isn't clear   1103
whether after all this care   1103a
they'll turn out well or badly.
Then there is one final drawback,   1105
the hardest thing of all to bear.
When the parents find a way
to give their children what they need
to grow up strong and honest,
but then luck turns: death scoops them up   1110
and carries their bodies down to Hades.
What possible good can it do
for the gods to impose on us
this bitter, bitter sorrow
as the price of having children?   1115

MEDEA   My friends, I have been waiting a long time now
    wondering how things would turn out in there.
    But now I see one of Jason's servants
    coming towards us. He is breathing hard,
    and it's clear he has something grim to report.   1120
        [*Enter the* MESSENGER.]
MESSENGER   [Oh you have done a dreadful, lawless thing]
    Run Medea! Run! Make your escape—
    get away in a ship or overland in a carriage.
MEDEA   And what has happened that means I should flee?
MESSENGER   The royal princess has fallen down dead,   1125
    along with her father, because of your poison.
MEDEA   You have brought the most wonderful news.

I will always think of you as a true friend.

MESSENGER   What are you saying? Are you out of your mind?
   You have desecrated the royal hearth,   1130
   and you're glad? Not terrified at what you've done?

MEDEA   I have things to say in response to that.
   But please do not rush through your report.
   How exactly did they die? You will make me
   twice as happy if they died horribly.   1135

MESSENGER   When your boys and their father
      first arrived
   at the new couple's house, there was great joy
   among the household slaves. We had been worried,
   but now a rumor was spreading through us
   that you and Jason had patched up your quarrel.   1140
   One kissed their hands, another their golden heads,
   and I in my happiness followed along
   into the women's rooms behind the children.
   The lady who had become our new mistress
   did not see at first that your sons were there;   1145
   she just gazed adoringly at Jason.
   But then suddenly she shut her eyes
   and turned her delicate face away,
   disgusted by the children's presence.
   But your husband calmed the girl down   1150
   saying, "They are family, don't reject them,
   let your anger go, look this way again;
   can't you treat your husband's kin as your own,
   accept their gifts, and ask your father
   to spare the boys from exile for my sake?"   1155
   She gave in when she saw those fine presents,
   and granted him everything he asked.
   As soon as the boys and their father had left,
   she seized that elegant dress and put it on;
   she placed the golden crown on her head   1160
   and arranged her hair in a shining mirror,
   smiling at her reflected features.
   Then she jumped up from her chair and ran
   all over the house on her little white feet,
   delighted with her presents; she kept looking down   1165
   to see how the dress fell against her ankle.
   But then we saw something truly horrible:
   her color changed; she staggered sideways
   on shaking legs; she nearly hit the ground
   as she fell backwards into a chair.   1170
   An older woman, thinking at first

that she was possessed by some god like Pan,[5]
raised a shout of joy. But then she saw
the foaming mouth, the skin drained of blood,
the eyeballs twisting in their sockets.   1175
She countered that shout of joy with a shriek
of woe. One slave girl rushed to the father's room;
another went straight to tell the husband
that his bride had collapsed. The whole house rang
with the sound of their frantic footsteps.   1180
In the time it would take a swift runner
to cover the last lap of a footrace,
she came out of her speechless, sightless trance
with an awful, chilling cry of pain.   1185
She was under a double assault:
the golden crown she had put in her hair
spewed out a torrent of consuming flames,
while those fine robes she got from your boys
were eating away at her pale flesh.
Burning alive, she leapt up from her chair   1190
and shook her head from side to side
trying to throw off the crown. But the bands
held tight, and all of her shaking
only made the fire blaze twice as high.
She gave up the struggle and fell to the floor.   1195
Only a parent would have known who she was.
You really couldn't make out her eyes
or the shape of her face. From the top of her head
blood mixed with fire was streaming down;
the flesh flowed off her bones like pine sap,   1200
loosened by the fangs of your unseen poison,
a horrible sight. No one wanted to touch
the corpse. Her fate taught us caution.
But her poor father came in without warning;
he entered the room and found the body.   1205
He began to wail and took it in his arms,
kissed it, and spoke to it: "My poor child,
what god has destroyed you in this cruel way,
making me lose you when I'm at death's door?
All I want is to die with you, dear child."   1210
When he stopped lamenting and tried to stand,
he got tangled up in those silky robes,
like a laurel shoot encircled by ivy.
It was a horrible sort of wrestling match:

5. Half-man, half-goat, a pastoral god associated with wild, ecstatic behavior.

he kept struggling to get up on his legs   1215
while she held him back. He pulled hard
but the flesh just came off his old bones.
In the end, he stopped fighting for his life,
worn out, no longer equal to the ordeal.
Two corpses lie there, the girl and her father   1220
[nearby, a disaster that cries out for tears].
I won't go into what this means for you;
you'll find out what penalty you have to pay.
The old truth comes home to me again:
human life is an empty shadow.   1225
People who believe themselves to be
the deepest thinkers are the biggest fools.
There isn't anyone who is truly blessed.
Rich people may be luckier than others
but I wouldn't really call them blessed.   1230

                              [*Exit the* MESSENGER.]

CHORUS   A god is giving Jason what he deserves:
   trouble after trouble in a single day.
   [Poor girl, poor daughter of Creon,
   I feel for you: you have been sent
   to Hades to pay for Jason's marriage.]   1235
MEDEA   Friends! My plan is clear: as fast as I can
   I will kill my sons and leave this land.
   I cannot hold back and let those boys
   be slaughtered by someone who loves them less.
   They have to die, so it is only right   1240
   that I who gave them life should kill them.
   Arm yourself, my heart! Don't hesitate
   to do the unavoidable awful thing.
   I must pick up the sword and step across
   the starting line of a painful course.   1245
   No weakening, no thoughts of the boys—
   how sweet they are, how you gave them birth.
   Forget your children for this one day;
   grieve afterwards. Even if you kill them,
   they still are loved—by you, unlucky woman.   1250

                              [*Exit* MEDEA *into the house.*]

CHORUS   Look, Mother Earth and Radiant Sun,
   look at this deadly woman,
   before she can raise her hand
   to spill the blood of her children,
   descendants of your golden line.
   I dread to think of immortal blood   1255

shed by mortal hands!
Hold her back, Zeus-born light! Make her stop!
Get this miserable murderous Fury
out of the house!   1260

All for nothing, your labor in childbirth,
all for nothing, your dearly-loved children,
you who passed through the perilous border
of the dark-faced Clashing Rocks.
Why has relentless anger   1265
settled in your heart,
why this rage for death upon death?
The stain of kindred blood weighs heavy.
The gods send the killers evil pains
to echo evil crimes.   1270

    FIRST BOY [*in the house*]
No! No!   1270a
CHORUS   Do you hear? Do you hear that child's cry?
    Oh that wretched, ill-starred woman!
FIRST BOY   Help! How do I get away from our mother?
SECOND BOY   I don't know how. There's no escape.
CHORUS   Should I go in? I might prevent   1275
    those boys from dying.
FIRST BOY   Yes, by the gods, yes! Help us now!
SECOND BOY   She has us cornered with her sword.
CHORUS   Wretched woman, made of stone, made of iron!
    I see you really have it in you   1280
    to turn your deadly hand
    against the boys you bore yourself.

    I have only heard of one other woman,
    who raised her hand against her children:
    Ino,[6] driven wild by Zeus's wife   1285
    who made her wander far from home.
    Poor woman, she plunged into the sea,
    and dragged her children to unholy death.
    Stepping over the seacliff's edge,
    she died along with her two sons.
    Is any dreadful thing impossible now?   1290
    How much disaster has been caused
    by the pain of women in marriage!

---

6. Wife of Athamas, king of Boeotia. To strengthen the parallel with Medea, Euripides is
reworking the usual version of the myth, in which Zeus's wife Hera drives Athamas mad,
he kills one of their children, and Ino falls off a cliff while fleeing with the other.

[*Enter* JASON.]

JASON   You women there beside the house,
   is Medea inside, the perpetrator
   of these terrible crimes? Has she escaped?   1295
   Unless she burrows deep in the earth
   or else grows wings and flies through the air,
   the royal family will make her pay.
   After she killed such powerful people,
   does she think she can escape scot-free?   1300
   Still, I'm mainly worried about the children.
   Those she abused can do the same to her,
   but I am here now to save my boys.
   More suffering for me if Creon's kinsmen
   try to punish them for their mother's crime.   1305
CHORUS   Poor man, you don't know all your troubles,
   or you would not have said what you just did.
JASON   What is it? Does she want to kill me too?
CHORUS   The boys are dead. Their mother killed them.
JASON   What are you saying? Those words are death
      to me.   1310
CHORUS   Don't think of your children as among the living.
JASON   She killed them . . . where? In the house or outside?
CHORUS   If you open the doors, you will see how they died.
JASON   Servants, draw back these bolts at once,
   open the doors, so I can see both evils: 1315
   the dead children and the woman I will punish.
      [*Enter* MEDEA *in a winged chariot above the house,*
      with the boys' bodies.]
MEDEA   Why do you keep banging on the doors
   to get at the boys and me, their killer?
   Don't exert yourself. If you have something to say,
   I'm here, go ahead. But you'll never touch me.   1320
   This chariot from my grandfather the Sun
   protects me from an enemy's hands.
JASON   You abomination, most hateful of women
   to the gods, to me, to the whole human race.
   You were actually able to drive a sword   1325
   into sons you had borne; you've made me childless.
   How can you live and see the light of the sun,
   when you have committed this sacrilege
   and ought to be dead? Now I see what I missed
   when I brought you from that barbarian place   1330
   into a Greek home. You are an evil being:
   you betrayed your father and your native land.

The gods are crushing me for what you did
when you killed your brother at the family hearth
before you boarded the beautiful *Argo*.   1335
That's how you started. Then you married me,
you bore me children and you killed them
just because of some sexual grievance.
No Greek woman would ever do that.
To think I bound myself to you instead   1340
in a hateful, ruinous union
with an inhuman wife, a lioness
more savage than Etruscan Scylla.[7]
All the angry words I could hurl at you   1345
carry no sting, you are so brazen.
To hell with you, you filthy child-killer!
All that is left for me is to mourn my fate;
I have lost the joy of my new marriage;
the children that I fathered and brought up
are gone. I'll never speak with them again.   1350

MEDEA   I could refute your speech at length,
but Father Zeus already knows
how you were treated by me and what you did.
There is no way you could reject my bed
and lead a happy life laughing at me,   1355
you or the princess, no way that Creon
who arranged all this could throw me out
and not pay the price. So call me a lion,
or Scylla lurking on the Etruscan plain,
I've done what I had to: I've pierced your heart.   1360

JASON   But it hurts you too, you share in this pain.

MEDEA   The pain is worth it if it kills your laughter.

JASON   O children, what a vicious mother you had!

MEDEA   O boys, your father's disease destroyed you!

JASON   It was not my hand that slaughtered them.   1365

MEDEA   No, your arrogance and your brand-new marriage.

JASON   You really think sex was a reason to kill them?

MEDEA   You think being spurned is trivial for a woman?

JASON   Yes, if she's sensible. You resent everything.

MEDEA   Well, they are gone, and that will bite deep.   1370

JASON   Oh, but they will take revenge on you.

MEDEA   The gods know which of us started this trouble.

JASON   Yes, they know your mind and it disgusts them.

---

7. A sea monster with six snake heads, positioned opposite the whirlpool Charybdis, who
   snatched sailors out of their ships.

MEDEA Hate all you want. I loathe the sound of your voice.
JASON And I loathe yours. We won't find it hard to part. 1375
MEDEA Then what's to be done? I too am eager for that.
JASON Let me bury these bodies and weep for them.
MEDEA Absolutely not. I will bury them myself
  in the shrine of Hera of the Rocky Heights,
  where none of my enemies can get at them 1380
  or wreck their graves. Here in the land of Sisyphus
  I will institute a procession and sacred rites
  as atonement for this unholy murder.
  Then I'll be off to the city of Erechtheus
  to live with Aegeus, Pandion's son. 1385
  You will have a fitting death for a coward,
  hit on the head by a piece of the *Argo*—
  the bitter result of marrying me.
JASON Let a Fury rise up to avenge these boys,
  and Justice that punishes bloodshed. 1390
MEDEA What god or spirit listens to you?
  You broke your oaths, you betrayed a friend!
JASON Ha! Abomination! Child-killer!
MEDEA Just go home and bury your wife.
JASON I am going, and without my children. 1395
MEDEA This grief is nothing. Wait till you're old.
JASON O children, much loved!
MEDEA   By their mother, not you.
JASON You, who killed them?
MEDEA   To punish you.
JASON All I want is to hold them tight,
  to press their sweet faces to mine. 1400
MEDEA Now you talk to them, now you kiss them.
  Before you shoved them aside.
JASON   By the gods,
  just let me touch their tender skin.
MEDEA Not possible. Your words are useless.
JASON Zeus, do you hear? I am shut out, 1405
  dismissed by this vicious animal,
  this lioness stained with children's blood.
  With all my being I grieve for them
  and summon the gods to witness
  how you destroyed my children, 1410
  and will not let me touch their bodies
  or bury them in proper tombs.
  I wish I had never fathered them
  to see them slaughtered by you.

[*Exit* MEDEA *in the chariot.*]

CHORUS   In all that Olympian Zeus watches over,   1415
   much is accomplished that we don't foresee.
   What we expect does not come about;
   the gods clear a path for the unexpected.
   That is how things happened here.[8]

8. The chorus's final lines appear in almost the same form in four other plays of Euripides, which has led some scholars to conclude that they are spurious.

CONTEXTS

XENOPHON

From Oeconomicus 7.1–30, 42–43[†]

The *Oeconomicus* is a treatise on household management in the form of a fictional philosophical dialogue, written around 360 B.C.E. (about seventy years after *Medea*). The philosopher Socrates is depicted as describing a conversation with an exemplary Athenian householder, Ischomachos, about his successful life and especially his marriage. The idealized picture that Ischomachos paints of an asymmetrical but mutually respectful lifelong bond, arranged between himself and his wife's parents, gives a sense of the cultural norms and expectations against which the marriage of Jason and Medea should be measured.

VII

(1) "Seeing him then one day sitting in the colonnade of Zeus the Deliverer, I went over to him, and as he seemed to be at leisure, I sat down with him and spoke. 'Why are you sitting like this, Ischomachos, you who are so unaccustomed to leisure? For I mostly see you either doing something or at least hardly at leisure in the market place.'

(2) "'Nor would you see me now, Socrates,' said Ischomachos, 'if I hadn't made an appointment to meet some foreigners here.'

"'When you aren't doing this sort of thing,' I said, 'by the gods, how do you spend your time and what do you do? For I would like very much to inquire what it is you do in order to be called a gentleman, since you don't spend your time indoors, and the condition of your body hardly looks like that of one who does.'

(3) "And Ischomachos, laughing at my asking what he did to be called a gentleman and rather pleased, or so it seemed to me, spoke. 'I don't know whether some call me by that name when discussing me with you, but surely when they call me to an exchange[1] for the support of a trireme or the training of a chorus, no one,' he said, 'goes looking for "the gentleman," but they summon me clearly,' he said, 'by the name Ischomachos and by my father's name.[2] As to what you asked me, Socrates,' he said, 'I never spend time indoors. Indeed,' he said, 'my wife·is quite able by herself to manage the things within the house.'

† From Leo Strauss, *Xenophon's Socratic Discourse: An Interpretation of the Oeco-nomicus*, trans. Carnes Lord, ed. Leo Strauss (Ithaca: Cornell UP, 1970), pp. 28–33, 35–36. Copyright © 1970 by Cornell University. Used by permission of the publisher, Cornell University Press. Notes by Lord.
1. *Antidosis.* There was an Athenian law according to which a man charged with a public duty could challenge someone he believed richer than himself either to take on the duty or to exchange his property for that of the challenger.
2. I.e., by his patronymic: "Ischomachos, the son of. . . ."

(4) "'It would please me very much, Ischomachos,' I said, 'if I might also inquire about this—whether you yourself educated your wife to be the way she ought to be, or whether, when you took her from her mother and father, she already knew how to manage the things that are appropriate to her.'[3]

(5) "'How, Socrates,' he said, 'could she have known anything when I took her, since she came to me when she was not yet fifteen, and had lived previously under diligent supervision in order that she might see and hear as little as possible and ask the fewest possible questions? (6) Doesn't it seem to you that one should be content if she came knowing only how to take the wool and make clothes, and had seen how the spinning work is distributed among the female attendants? For as to matters of the stomach, Socrates,' he said, 'she came to me very finely educated; and to me, at any rate, that seems to be an education of the greatest importance both for a man and a woman.'

(7) "'And in other respects, Ischomachos,' I said, 'did you yourself educate your wife to be capable of concerning herself with what's appropriate to her?'

"'By Zeus,' said Ischomachos, 'not until I had sacrificed and prayed that I might succeed in teaching, and she in learning, what is best for both of us.'

(8) "'Didn't your wife sacrifice with you and pray for these same things?' I said.

"'Certainly,' said Ischomachos; 'she promised before the gods that she would become what she ought to be, and made it evident that she would not neglect the things she was being taught.'

(9) "'By the gods, Ischomachos,' I said, 'relate to me what you first began teaching her. I'd listen to you relating these things with more pleasure than if you were telling me about the finest contest in wrestling or horsemanship.'

(10) "And Ischomachos replied: 'Well, Socrates,' he said, 'when she had gotten accustomed to me and had been domesticated to the extent that we could have discussions, I questioned her somewhat as follows. "Tell me, woman, have you thought yet why it was that I took you and your parents gave you to me? (11) That it was not for want of someone else to spend the night with—this is obvious, I know, to you too. Rather, when I considered for myself, and your parents for you, whom we might take as the best partner for the household and children, I chose you, and your parents, as it appears, from among the possibilities[4] chose me. (12) Should a god grant us children, we will then consider, with respect to them, how we may

---

3. The expression can also mean "the things that belong to her."
4. The expression could also mean either "from among capable men," i.e., men of some wealth and position, or "according to their [i.e., the parents'] capabilities."

best educate them; for this too is a good common to us—to obtain the best allies and the best supporters in old age; (13) but for the present this household is what is common to us. As to myself, everything of mine I declare to be in common, and as for you, everything you've brought you have deposited in common. It's not necessary to calculate which of us has contributed the greater number of things, but it is necessary to know this well, that whichever of us is the better partner will be the one to contribute the things of greater worth." (14) To this, Socrates, my wife replied: "What can I do to help you?" she said. "What is my capacity? But everything depends on you: my work, my mother told me, is to be moderate." (15) "By Zeus, woman," I said, "my father told me the same thing. But it's for moderate people—for man and woman alike—not only to keep their substance in the best condition but also to add as much as possible to it by fine and just means." (16) "Then what do you see," said my wife, "that I might do to help in increasing the household?" "By Zeus," I said, "just try to do in the best manner possible what the gods have brought you forth to be capable of and what the law praises." (17) "And what are these things?" she said. "I suppose they are things of no little worth," I said, "unless, of course, the leading bee in the hive also has charge of works of little worth. (18) For it seems to me, woman,"' he said that he had said, '"that the gods have used great consideration in joining together the pair called male and female so that it may be of the greatest benefit to itself in its community. (19) First, that the races of living things may not be extinguished, the pair is brought together for the production of children; then, from this pairing it is given to human beings at least to possess supporters in old age; but then the way of life of human beings is not, as is that of cattle, in the open air, but evidently needs shelter. (20) Still, if human beings are going to have something to bring into the dwellings, someone is needed to work in the open air. For plowing the fallow, sowing, planting, and herding are all works of the open air, and from them the necessary things are gotten. (21) But when these things have been brought into the dwelling, someone is needed to keep them secure and to do the works that need shelter. The rearing of newborn children also needs shelter; shelter is needed for the making of bread from the crop, and similarly for the working of clothes from wool. (22) Since, then, work and diligence are needed both for the indoor and for the outdoor things, it seems to me,"' he had said, '"that the god directly prepared the woman's nature for indoor works and indoor concerns.[5] (23) For he equipped the man,

5. The construction of this sentence in Greek could lead one to believe that something has dropped out of the text at this point. The Oxford editor makes the following conjecture, which, however, lacks manuscript authority: "and that of the man for outdoor ones."

in body and in soul, with a greater capacity to endure cold and heat, journeys and expeditions, and so has ordered him to the outdoor works; but in bringing forth, for the woman, a body that is less capable in these respects,"' he said that he had said, '"the god has, it seems to me, ordered her to the indoor works. (24) But knowing that he had implanted[6] in the woman, and ordered her to, the nourishment of newborn children, he also gave her a greater affection for the newborn infants than he gave to the man. (25) Since he had also ordered the woman to the guarding of the things brought in, the god, understanding that a fearful soul is not worse at guarding, also gave the woman a greater share of fear than the man. And knowing too that the one who had the outdoor works would need to defend himself should someone act unjustly, to him he gave a greater share of boldness. (26) But because it's necessary for both to give and to take, he endowed both with memory and diligence in like degree, so that you can't distinguish whether the male or the female kind has the greater share of these things. (27) As for self-control in the necessary things, he endowed both with this too in like degree; and the god allowed the one who proved the better, whether the man or the woman, to derive more from this good. (28) Since, then, the nature of each has not been brought forth to be naturally apt for all of the same things, each has need of the other, and their pairing is more beneficial to each, for where one falls short the other is capable. (29) Now," I said, "O woman, as we know what has been ordered to each of us by the god, we must, separately, do what's appropriate to each. (30) The law too praises these things,"' he said that he had said, '"in pairing man and woman; and as the god made them partners in children, so too does the law appoint them partners.[7] And the law shows that what the god has brought forth each to be capable of is fine as well. It is a finer thing for the woman to stay indoors than to spend time in the open, while it is more disgraceful for the man to stay indoors than to concern himself with outdoor things * * * (42) But the most pleasant thing of all: if you look to be better than I and make me your servant, you will have no need to fear that with advancing age you will be honored any less in the household, and you may trust that as you grow older, the better a partner you prove to be for me, and for the children the better a guardian of the household, by so much more will you be honored in the household. (43) For the fine and good things increase for human beings, not by ripening like fair fruits,[8] but through the

---

6. The words for "implant" and "bring forth" have the same root, being related to the word for "nature" (*physis*).
7. In the Oxford text this phrase is emended to read, in translation: "so too does the law appoint them partners in the household." The insertion of the words for "in the household" is without manuscript authority.
8. "Ripening like fair fruits" translates *ōraiotēs*, a word of rare occurrence and uncertain meaning. It suggests seasonableness, ripeness, and beauty.

exercise of the virtues in life," I seem to remember saying such things
to her, Socrates, at the time of our first discussion." "

APOLLONIUS OF RHODES

From Argonautica 3.744–824[†]

The *Argonautica* is an epic poem composed around 240 B.C.E. (200 years
after Euripides' *Medea*) that tells the story of the Argonauts' quest for the
Golden Fleece, beginning with Pelias's challenge and ending with their
return to Greece. Apollonius and his well-educated audience were familiar with Euripides' play, and the *Argonautica* is self-consciously framed as
the backstory to *Medea*. Medea's indispensable role in Jason's success is
central to the narrative, which includes a detailed portrait of her state
of mind as a young girl overwhelmed by love. In this passage, Apollonius gives Medea (here spelled Medeia) an anguished inner debate over
whether she should abandon her parents and help Jason that anticipates
her debate over killing her children in *Medea*. Medea's close association
with drugs and the ominous reference to a mother whose children are
dead also evoke her later career as portrayed in that famous earlier work.

* * *

Night soon darkened the earth, and out on Ocean
sailors looked up from their ships to the stars of Orion   745
and the Great Bear, while travelers and gate porters
longed for a chance to sleep, and a profound torpor
enveloped some mother whose children had all perished:
throughout the city even the dogs ceased their barking,
human voices fell silent: stillness possessed the
    deepening gloom.   750
But on Medeia sweet sleep could get no hold, kept
wakeful as she was by worrying over Jason
in her longing for him, and dreading the great might
    of the bulls
that would bring him an ill fate there on Ares' ploughland.
Close and quick now beat the heart in her bosom,   755
as a shaft of sunlight will dance along the house wall
when flung up from water new-poured into pail or cauldron:
hither and thither the swiftly circling ripples
send it darting, a *frisson* of brightness; in just such a way
her virgin heart now beat a tattoo on her ribs,   760

† From *The Argonautika*, trans. Peter Green (Berkeley: U of California P, 1997),
   pp. 132–34. © 1997 by Peter Green. Reprinted by permission of the University of California Press.

her eyes shed tears of pity, constant anguish
ran smoldering through her flesh, hot-wired her finespun
nerve ends, needled into the skull's base, the deep spinal
cord where pain pierces sharpest when the unresting
passions inject their agony into the senses.   765
Her mind veered: now she thought she'd give him
    the magic stuff
to quell the bulls; now not, but would herself die with him;
then the next moment that she'd neither help him nor perish,
but rather just stay put, and bear her fate in silence.
Finally, indecisive, she sat herself down and said: 770
"Wretch that I am, I'm for trouble, one way or the other—
my mind lacks any resource, there's no sure remedy
for this pain of mine, it burns without cess: how I wish
I'd been killed already by the swift shafts of Artemis
before I'd ever set eyes on him, before Chalkíope's sons[1]   775
had gone to Achaia: it was a god or some Fury
brought them thence hither, for us sore grief and weeping.
Let the contest destroy him, then, if it's his destiny
to die on that ploughland! For how could I set up my magic
drugs and my parents not know it? What tale can I tell them?   780
What deception, what crafty scheme will there be to help me?
How catch him alone, approach him, away from
    his companions?
And suppose him dead—not even thus can I hope, with my
bad luck, for relief from these sorrows: it's then,
    when bereft of life,
that he'd do me most grievous harm. . . . Ah, let modesty
    go hang,   785
and my good name with it! Saved by my intervention
let him take off, unharmed, for anywhere he chooses—
and then, the very day that he triumphs in his contest,
may I find death, either stretching my neck from a roofbeam
or swallowing drugs that destroy the human spirit.   790
Yet even so, when I'm dead, there'll be nods
    and winks, reproaches
at my expense, the whole city will broadcast my fate
far and wide, my name will be common coin, bandied
to and fro, with vile insults, on the lips of our Kolchian
women—"This girl who cared so much for some foreign   795
man that she died, this girl who shamed home and parents,

---

1. Chalkiope is Medea's sister; her sons have joined the Argonauts, and she has been urging
   Medea to help them.

overcome by sheer lust—" What reproach shall I not suffer?
With my blind infatuation would it not be better
this very night to slough life off, here in my chamber,
a sudden end, unexplained, and so escape all censure,   800
before committing such deeds, unspeakable, infamous?"
With that she fetched out a casket, in which were stored
drugs of all kinds, some healing, others destructive,
and setting it on her knees she wept, raining endless
tears down over her bosom, a flood, a torrent,   805
as she bitterly mourned her fate. A yearning seized her
to choose some lethal drug, and then to drink it,
and she actually started to lift the hasps of the casket,
poor girl, in her eagerness; but then, on a sudden,
a deathly fear gripped her heart of loathsome Hades,   810
and long she froze, numb and speechless, while around her
all life's delectable cares caressed her vision.
She remembered the many delights that exist among
    the living,
she remembered her happy companions, as a young girl will,
and the Sun grew sweeter to look on than ever before   815
once she truly reached out to all these things with her mind.
The casket she raised from her lap and put away once more,
transformed by the promptings of Hera, wavering no longer
between decisions, but impatient for dawn to break
quickly, that moment, so she could give him the spellbinding   820
charms as she'd covenanted, and meet him face to face.
Time and again she unbolted and opened her door
watching for first light, and happy she was when daybreak
brightened the sky, and folk began stirring in the city.

*   *   *

SENECA

From Medea 891–1001[†]

Seneca's *Medea* is a tragedy written in Latin in around 50 C.E. (about
500 years after Euripides' play) by the Roman poet and philosopher Seneca. Seneca's play is partly based on Euripides' version but differs significantly in ways that make it more sensational: Medea is a full-blown

---

[†] From *Seneca: Six Tragedies*, trans. Emily Wilson (Oxford and New York: Oxford UP,
2010), pp. 97–101. Reprinted by permission of Oxford University Press. Notes are by
the editor of this Norton Critical Edition.

witch whose extensive use of magic is described in detail, her previous
crimes are repeatedly evoked, her killing of the children is portrayed
directly (although it is not known whether the play was actually staged),
and there is a greater emphasis throughout on the passions that drive
her. In addition, Medea is conscious of herself as a theatrical figure,
aware of her own place in literary tradition and interested in her own
acts as spectacles. In this passage from the end of the play, Medea
chooses to kill her sons as an act that will make her truly "Medea," sacrifices one of them to the fury of her dead brother, and prepares for the
murder of the other as a tormenting sight for Jason to watch.

ACT FIVE

* * *

NURSE   Carry yourself away, fast as you can,
      from the land of Pelops,
   Medea, run away: find anywhere else to live.
MEDEA   I? Would I run? Would I yield? If I had fled before
   I would return for this, to watch a new type of wedding.
   Why hesitate, my soul? Follow your lucky strike.
   This is a tiny fraction of your triumph.
   You are still in love, mad heart, if this is enough:
   to see Jason unmarried. Look for new punishment,
   unprecedented, and prepare yourself:
   let all morality be gone, and exile shame;   900
   that vengeance is too light which clean hands can perform.
   Spur on your anger, rouse your weary self,
   from the depths of your heart draw up your former passions
   with even greater violence. Whatever I did before,
   name it dutiful love. Come now! I will reveal
   how trivial and ordinary they were,
   those crimes I did before. With them, my bitterness
   was only practising: how could my childish hands
   do something truly great? Could the rage of a girl do this?
   Now, I am Medea. My nature has grown with my suffering.   910
   I am happy that I ripped my brother's head away,
   I am glad I sliced his limbs, and glad I stripped my father
   of his ancestral treasure,[1] I am glad I set on the daughters
   to murder the old man.[2] Now, pain, find your new chance.
   You bring to every action a hand that knows its way.
   Where then, my anger, shall I point you? Fire what weapons
   at that traitor? My savage heart has made a plan,
   a secret one, stored deep inside, and does not dare

---

1. The Golden Fleece.
2. Pelias, Jason's hostile uncle, whom Medea killed by persuading his daughters that they
   could make him immortal by putting him in a pot of boiling water.

reveal it yet, even to itself. Fool! I went too fast.
I wish my enemy had had some children   920
by that concubine of his.—Whatever was yours by him,
Creusa was its mother. That kind of punishment
is what I want; yes, good. My great heart must do
the final wickedness. Children—once my children—
you must give yourselves as payback for your father's crimes.
     Awful! It hits my heart, my body turns to ice,
my chest is heaving. Anger has departed,
the wife in me is gone, I am all mother again.
Is this me? Could I spill my own children's blood,
flesh of my flesh? No, no, what terrible madness!   930
Let that horrible deed, that dreadful crime,
     be unthought of,
even by me. Poor things! What crime have they
     ever done?—
Jason is their father: that is their crime. And worse:
Medea is their mother. Let them die; they are not mine.
Let them die; they are mine. They did nothing wrong,
     they are blameless,
they are innocent: I admit it. So was my brother.
Why, my soul, do you waver? Why are my cheeks
     blotched with tears,
why am I led in two directions, now by anger,
now by love? My double inclination tears me apart.
As when the wild winds make their brutal wars   940
and on both sides the seas lift up discordant waves,
and the unstable water boils: even so my heart
tosses and churns: love is chased out by rage
and rage by love. Resentment, yield to love.
     Here to me, darling children, only comfort
for this troubled house, bring yourselves here, embrace me,
fold yourselves in my arms. Let your father have you safe,
as long as your mother has you too.—But I must go
     in exile.
Any minute, they will be ripped from my arms,
weeping and wailing. Let their father lose their kisses,   950
their mother has already lost them. Again, my anger grows,
my hatred boils. My ancient Fury seeks
my reluctant hands again—anger, I follow your lead.
I wish as many children as proud Niobe[3] bore

3. Boasted that she had more children (fourteen) than the goddess Leto, who had only
two, Apollo and Diana (the Roman equivalent of the Greek Artemis). Apollo and Diana
took revenge by killing all of Niobe's children; she wept so much that she turned to stone.

had come from my womb, I wish I had
twice-seven sons! I was infertile for revenge:
but my two are just enough to pay for brother and father.
Look! What are they doing, this violent crowd of Furies?
Whom are they seeking, at whom are they aiming
   those flaming blows,
at whom does the hellish army aim its bloody torches?   960
The great snake hisses and twists as the whip comes down.
Whom is the head of the Furies seeking,
   with her menacing brand,
Megaera? Whose shade comes half-invisible, his limbs
scattered apart? It is my brother, he wants revenge.
We will pay it: we will all pay. Fix deep your torch
   in my eyes,
ravage me, burn me up, see, my whole breast is open
   for the Furies.
   Leave me, my brother, and you avenging goddesses,
and order your ghosts to go back safe to the depths of Hell.
Leave me to myself and use this hand, my brother,
which has drawn the sword: we appease your spirit now,   970
with this sacrificial victim.—What was that sudden noise?
They are taking up weapons against me, they want
   to kill me.
I will climb up to the topmost roof of our house
though the killing is unfinished. All of you, come with me.
And I myself will carry away with me your body.
Now do it, heart: you must not waste your courage
in secret: prove to the people the things you can do.

JASON   If any man is loyal, and mourns the princes' death,
   run, gather here, let us arrest that wicked woman
   who did the dreadful crime. Come, my brave band
     of warriors,   980
   bring here your weapons, push her from the top of
     the house.

MEDEA   Now, now I have regained my throne, my brother,
   and my father.
The Colchians keep the treasure of the Golden Ram.
My kingdom comes back to me, my stolen virginity returns.
O gods, you favour me at last, O happy day,
O wedding day! Now leave, the crime is complete:
I am not yet revenged. Go on, while you are at it:
Why do you hesitate now, my soul? Why are you doubtful?
Does your powerful anger now subside?
   I am sorry for what I have done,

I am ashamed. What, wretch, have you done? Wretch?   990
    Even if I regret it,
I have done it. Great pleasure steals over me against
    my will,
and see! now it grows. This was all I was missing,
that Jason should be watching. I think I have so far
    done nothing:
crimes committed without him were wasted.

JASON   Look, she is hovering on the outermost part
    of the roof.
Somebody, bring fire, and burn her up, let her fall
consumed by her own flames.

MEDEA   Heap up a funeral pyre
    for your own sons, Jason, and strew the burial mound.
    your wife and father-in-law now have their proper rites: 1000
    I have buried them. This son has already met his fate;
    this one will die the same, but you will watch.

*   *   *

CRITICISM

P. E. EASTERLING

The Infanticide in Euripides' *Medea*[†]

In many respects Euripides' *Medea* is not a problematic play. It is a singularly bold, clear-cut, assured piece of writing, the concentration and dramatic intensity of which are readily felt by reader or audience and command the respect even of those who find the subject matter repellent or who cavil at the Aegeus scene and the dragon chariot. But its starkness makes it deeply disturbing; and this unease is reflected in the critical literature on the play. The language, though consistently powerful, lacks the rich expansiveness of *Hippolytus* or *Bacchae*, almost never allowing us to range in imagination away from the immediate painful situation; it is typical that one of the most prominent of the recurring images is of Medea as a wild beast.[1] Then there is the striking absence of a cosmic frame of reference: we are given no sense of divine motivation or sanction or control. Medea is admittedly grand-daughter of the Sun, but the fact has no theological significance: its function is to symbolize her sense of her heroic identity and—at a different level— to motivate the final scene. The most uncompromising feature of all is Euripides' handling of the story, his design which makes the murder of the children the centrepiece of the play.

This horrific act is something from which we naturally recoil. 'No sane person', we say, 'would do such a thing', and indeed Euripides' many imitators have tended to present Medea's behaviour as that of a madwoman.[2] Or 'no civilized person would do it'; Sir Denys Page, for example, writes, 'The murder of children . . . is mere brutality: if it moves us at all, it does so towards incredulity and horror. Such an act is outside our experience, we—and the fifth-century Athenian— know nothing of it.'[3] Doubts have been felt in particular about Medea's great speech at 1021ff. in which she wrestles with her conflicting feelings of injured pride and love for her children: is Euripides merely playing with our emotions through a rhetorical handling of the situation, exploiting the dramatic effectiveness of Medea's debate with herself rather than having an eye to what a person would really do in such circumstances?[4] Or conversely, is this conflict in

---

[†] From *Yale Classical Studies* 25 (1977): 177–91. Copyright © 1977 Cambridge University Press. Reprinted by permission of Cambridge University Press. Notes and translations in brackets are by the editor of this Norton Critical Edition.
1. 92; (103); 187ff.; 1342f.; 1358f.; 1407.
2. Cf. W. H. Friedrich, 'Medeas Rache' in *Euripides*, ed. E.-R. Schwinge (Darmstadt 1968), p. 209.
3. D. L. Page, *Euripides, Medea* (Oxford 1938), p. xiv.
4. 'She has her struggle with her maternal feelings—a theatrical struggle rather than a psychologically convincing one', H. D. F. Kitto, *Greek Tragedy*, 3rd ed. (London 1961), p. 195.

Medea's soul the real high point of the drama, of more tragic importance than the violent act itself?[5] Or is it possible, as has recently
been suggested, that we retain some sympathy with Medea right
through to her final triumph, so that the final scene is the real climax of the play?[6] Clearly an important question to be faced by any
critic who wishes to interpret *Medea* is whether Euripides is explor-
ing the realities of human behaviour or creating only an illusion of
reality out of a sequence of essentially melodramatic actions.

'Real life' in drama is not, of course, the same phenomenon as real
life outside. Distortion or suppression of documentary fact and
neglect—within certain limits—even of probability are part of the
dramatist's stock-in-trade which we accept at the same time as believing in the truthfulness of his situations. Thus it is no fundamental
failure on Euripides' part that he abandons probability in his treatment of the chorus. It is highly unlikely that these respectable ladies
of Corinth would really have stood ineffectually by when Medea
announced her intention to kill their king and princess and then her
own children. In real life they would have taken steps to have Medea
taken into custody, or at the very least would have gone to warn the
royal family and Jason. But we accept their inactivity because these
women are not at the centre of the play: they are peripheral figures
whose role is not to do and suffer but to comment, sympathize, support or disapprove. The advantages of providing Medea with a sympathetic and understanding audience within the play far outweigh
any loss of naturalism. A much graver breach is committed by Seneca, when he makes Medea after killing the children toss the corpses
down to Jason.[7] The whole motivation of the mother who murders
her children is unintelligible if she is willing to surrender their corpses
to the husband whom she is punishing. Similarly, in Corneille's
Médée there is no conviction at all in the scene where *Jason* thinks of
killing the children to punish Medea.[8]

It is worth considering how Euripides manipulates the story in
order to force us to take Medea seriously. The barbarian sorceress
with a melodramatic criminal record who could so easily be a monster must become a tragic character, a paradigm, in some sense, of
humanity. The Nurse's opening speech alludes briefly to that record: Medea is in exile for persuading the daughters of Pelias to kill
their father, but there is no suggestion that she is shunned or feared
by the Corinthians; the Nurse says she 'pleases' them (11f.) and the
friendly words of the chorus (137, 178ff.) imply that she is an

---

5. Cf. M. Pohlenz, *Die griechische Tragödie*, 2nd ed. (Göttingen 1954), vol. 1, pp. 255ff.
6. So W. Steidle, *Studien zum Antiken Drama* (Munich 1968), p. 165.
7. If modern editors are right in so interpreting 'recipe iam natos parens' ['now, Father, take your children back'] (*Medea* 1024).
8. *Médée* V. v.

accepted, even a respected, figure. According to a scholiast [an ancient critic] on Pindar (*Olympian Odes* 13. 74) Medea served the Corinthians by stopping a famine in their city; but Euripides makes no explicit mention of a story which on the face of it looks ideally suited to his purpose, for the good reason that it would introduce distracting complications into the scene with Creon. Unlike Seneca and Corneille, he clearly wanted to avoid giving the situation even the vaguest political dimension: there are to be no outside pressures on Creon, and he is to have no obligations to Medea for past services. So Euripides with fine sleight-of-hand contrives to imply that Medea's status at Corinth is one of some dignity, but without explaining why; later it becomes clear that she has a reputation as a wise woman, but the picture that is very lightly sketched in (for example in the scene with Aegeus) is as close to that of a respectable religious authority as to that of an outlandish witch.[9]

Medea as foreigner is another theme which is delicately handled by Euripides. At the most superficial level the fact that she is a barbarian from Colchis must have helped a Greek audience to accept both her past crimes and her expertise as a powerful sorceress, but we should be rash to conclude that it offered them an adequate explanation of the child murder. If Medea is to be seen as a distinctively oriental type ('because she was a foreigner she could kill her children'[1]) why does Euripides make her talk like a Greek, argue like a Greek, and to all appearances *feel* like a Greek? It is hard to believe, particularly in view of the astonishingly crass words he gives to Jason at 536ff., that Euripides was seriously imputing moral superiority to the Greeks, implying that only a foreigner could or would murder her own kin. On the contrary, he seems to exploit the theme of Medea's foreignness in order to emphasize her vulnerability and isolation and also to make a searching analysis of the nature of civilization and barbarism, a deep preoccupation of this play, to which we shall return.

Similarly, the record of Medea's past crimes is used—initially at any rate—more to arouse than to alienate the audience's sympathy. Euripides does not suppress the murder of Apsyrtus (166–7) or the killing of Pelias (9), though he is careful not to dwell on the grisly details of dismemberment and boiling. The subdued recall of these past horrors no doubt foreshadows the violence to come; but one of its main functions is to make clear that Medea has sacrificed literally everything for Jason, thus emphasizing his special ingratitude and her special defencelessness: she has not merely abandoned her family, she has betrayed them for Jason's sake. Nor does Euripides allow any character to raise the question of the legal relationship between

9. Cf. D. J. Conacher, *Euripidean Drama* (Toronto 1967), pp. 186–7, 190.
1. Page (n. 3 above), p. xxi.

Jason and Medea. None of them suggests[2] that Jason was perfectly entitled to abandon Medea without bad faith because as a foreigner she could not be his legitimate wife. Like other dramatists in other plays[3] Euripides permits himself a certain vagueness in legal matters, relying on the fact that the story is set in the heroic age, not in fifth-century Athens, however strongly the social comment may strike us as contemporary. This is one of those questions which in real life would be crucially important, but which it suits a dramatist to suppress. The essential situation is perfectly clear-cut: Jason and Medea are to be regarded as permanently pledged,[4] so that when Jason abandons Medea he *is* breaking faith (and even he does not deny it).

Euripides has taken pains, therefore, to present the situation in such a way that we are obliged to take Medea seriously. The structure of the first part of the play and the detail of these early scenes seem to be aimed at the same objective, the audience's full response to Medea as a tragic character.

The prologue from 46ff., the entry of the children, can fairly be described as a 'mirror scene', a tightly self-contained presentation in miniature of the course that the action is going to take. It has very little direct connection with the immediately following scene, beyond the fact that the chorus ask the Nurse to coax Medea out of the house and she does actually emerge at 214, the beginning of the first episode; its main function seems rather to be prophetic, like the short scene in *Hippolytus* where the old servant reproves Hippolytus for his neglect of Aphrodite (88–120). Here the Nurse three times expresses her fear for the children's safety at their mother's hands (90ff.; 100ff.; 116ff.), having already glancingly introduced the theme in her opening speech: 'She hates the children and takes no pleasure in seeing them. I am afraid she may make some new [i.e. sinister] plan' (36f.). Medea's own curses reinforce this sense of foreboding: 'O cursed children of a hateful mother, may you perish with your father, and the whole house go to ruin!' (112ff.). And the children themselves appear, fresh from their games, to impress their significance on the audience. From the start, then, it is made clear that this is not just a quarrel between man and wife, but a family drama in which the future and even the safety of the children are at stake. Medea herself is presented in all the alarming violence of her passion, but framed by the sympathy of Nurse and chorus, and therefore to be seen by the audience as a victim, even if also as a potential criminal.

2. Although at least one critic has done so (G. Murray, in the introduction to his translation (London 1910), pp. viif.).
3. E.g. Sophocles on the edict in *Antigone*. Cf. D. A. Hester, *Mnemosyne* 24 (1971), 19–21.
4. The theme of their oaths is given repeated stress: 21ff.; 160ff.; 168ff.; 208ff.; 438ff. (and the whole *stasimon*); 492ff.; 1392.

When Medea comes out to talk to the chorus all the wildness has gone and she develops her arguments with complete composure. The focus of the dramatic interest is now this commanding personality in a sequence of encounters, first with the chorus, then with three men who in different ways have power to affect her life. With the chorus she is at her most frank and open, winning their whole-hearted support with her account of the miseries of a woman's life. At this stage the audience, too, must readily give her their sympathy, but complications already begin to arise. How much, we may ask, of what she says to the chorus is special pleading, designed to make them promise to keep her secret? As always with Medea it is hard to be sure; and here we meet for the first time the subtle complexity of Euripides' character-portrayal. At least her description of the constraints on women is deeply convincing, but when she complains of her special lack of resource as a foreigner with 'no mother, no *brother*, no kinsman' to support her (257f.) we perhaps remember that it was she herself who caused her brother's death and betrayed her family. These words lead straight into her plea for collusion on the part of the chorus if she finds some way of punishing her husband: 'for woman is fearful and timid in other respects and a coward when it comes to looking on steel, but when her marriage is treated with contempt there is no bloodier purpose than hers' (263ff.). We are left in no doubt that this is a formidable woman; and, despite all that she has said in this scene about the limitations of the feminine role, it is clear that she herself is capable of overcoming them. When she makes her famous claim (250f.) that she would rather stand three times in the battle line than bear one child she wins our respect—she is talking, of course, about the emotional hazards of being a mother, not just about the physical pain and danger of childbearing—but even so, not many women would say what Medea says; these words may come back to our minds at the end of the scene with Creon.

With the king we see the full exposure of Medea's cleverness, her *sophia*. Creon is explicit that he is exiling her because he fears what her cleverness may devise to harm his family; Medea's response is a dazzling virtuoso display of the very quality he fears. First she argues that her cleverness could not possibly be used to harm *him*, next exerts extreme emotional pressure by appealing to his feelings as a father,[5] and finally makes a disarmingly modest request: just one day's grace, time for making the necessary arrangements for going into exile. But as soon as he has left and Medea has got her way there is a striking change of tone: now we see all the contempt of the clever

5. E. Schlesinger, *Hermes* 94 (1966), 42, makes much of Creon's remark at 329 that his children are dearer to him than anything else in life. This is certainly important, in that it gives Medea her cue for exploiting Creon and keeps the theme of children in the foreground, but can we say that it actually gives her the idea of killing her children?

person for the fool. 'Do you think I would have fawned on that man if I had not had some profit or plan in mind?' (368f.). Now in a highly professional way she discusses the possible modes of murder she might choose: shall it be fire, or sword, or poison, her speciality? This could easily be bloodcurdling for bloodcurdling's sake as in Seneca and Corneille, who both make much of her gruesome rites and incantations. In Euripides the effect is less gothic; indeed a main function of this detail seems to be to emphasize Medea's cleverness: in her own view of herself her magical skill is part of her heroic *arete* [excellence].

This speech at 364ff. (and particularly the last section from 392) illuminates a most important aspect of Euripides' Medea. She sees herself not just as a woman wronged, but as a great personage in the heroic mould of an Ajax or an Achilles: she owes it to herself and to her high pedigree to allow no enemy to triumph over her. The granddaughter of Helios must face the test of courage: νῦν ἀγὼν εὐψυχίας ['you approach the act that will test your spirit'], language that an Ajax or an Achilles might perfectly well use. In this context Medea standing in the battle line becomes fully intelligible. The scene ends on a less grandiose, more sinister, note: 'We are women, helpless when it comes to good deeds, but skilled practitioners of all kinds of evil' (408f.).[6] There is a clash here between Medea's self-image as a hero of the old style braving a great ordeal and her awareness of the destructiveness of thwarted female passion. We see very clearly that her cleverness is a potent force for evil as well as for good. The tragedy is that she does stand out above the limited or shabby people around her, does have a sharper moral awareness and far greater distinction and force of personality, yet the audience cannot help but shudder at the ruthlessness of her anger and passion for vengeance.

In her first scene with Jason, Medea is at her most sympathetic, because here we are allowed to see the full extent of the provocation she has been suffering. Jason is a status-seeker, embarrassed by his barbarian wife who refuses to go quietly, anxious to have her out of the way but insensitive enough to talk about exile being a hardship, crassly patronizing in his offer of material help. Medea's theme is simple: 'I saved you';[7] and she is right. All her past acts of betrayal were committed in the cause of Jason and her love for him; and now he is guilty of the greatest betrayal of all, the breaking of those dearly-bought oaths. The only extenuation would have been if their union had been childless: but they *have children* (παίδων γεγώτων ['even though we have children'], at 490 carries the strongest possible emphasis). Jason's answer only confirms our sense of his outrageousness. He is sophistical in his argument that it was

---

6. The rhyme (ἀμηχανώταται, [*amêchanôtatai* 'most helpless'] . . . σοφώταται [*sophôtatai*, 'most skillful']) adds to the sonorousness of this ending.
7. 476; 515: powerful use of ring-composition.

Cypris [Aphrodite], not Medea, who saved him, ludicrously arrogant when he recalls the benefits he has conferred on his wife by bringing her to civilized Greece from her benighted barbarian home, patently self-deceptive[8] when he pretends that his only interest in the new marriage is the welfare of his existing family. Once more the importance of children is made very prominent, particularly at 565, when Jason implies that he needs a family more than Medea does. Medea's final taunt turns into a sinister threat which recalls the concluding lines of the two previous scenes: we are reminded that she is still planning revenge, though the encounter with Jason has done nothing to further the action in any practical sense and Medea still has no idea where she can go when she has punished her victims.

Then Aegeus arrives unexpectedly to answer her need. Aegeus is merely passing through Corinth on his way from the Delphic oracle to consult Pittheus, his old friend who is king of Troezen. The casualness of his arrival has been criticized from Aristotle[9] onwards, but as with Io's visit to the Caucasus in *Prometheus Bound* such casualness is readily acceptable to an audience provided that the scene itself is dramatically significant, and provided that it is seen to be part of a structural pattern. Here there is a clearly discernible design: three constrasting visits to Medea, of which the third offers a close parallel to the first.[1] Both the scene with Creon and the scene with Aegeus show Medea using her wits to get what she wants from a person in authority; but whereas Creon was all suspicion and misgivings Aegeus is full of honourable and rather naive trust. Medea is equal to either situation; and the most interesting link between the two scenes is in her choice of persuasive argument. With Creon it is his feelings as a parent she exploits, with Aegeus his longing to be a parent. Once more her cleverness succeeds: she now has a refuge in Athens, and she can afford to make a detailed plan of vengeance.

Her speech at 764ff. is the most remarkable in the play. It starts with her triumphant exultation and her plot for the murder of the princess and Creon, then leads without preparation into the terrible revelation that she intends to kill her children. Her own explanation makes the best starting point for a discussion of this speech. She sees the murder of her children as a means of *punishing her enemies*. The deed will be 'most unholy', but she will do it because her enemies' laughter is not to be tolerated. The penalty that is worse than death for her enemy Jason will be to have no children, neither Medea's nor any borne to him by the princess. And so 'let no one think me cowardly or weak, or peaceable, but of quite the opposite

---

8. The chorus are not deceived (578; 637ff.); and Jason's words to the princess (reported by the Messenger at 1151ff.) suggest that he was enjoying his role as royal bridegroom.
9. *Poetics* 1461 b 21. At least Euripides has warned us to expect *someone* to arrive (390–4).
1. Cf. D. W. Lucas, *The Greek Tragic Poets*, 2nd ed. (London 1959), p. 197.

temper: dire to my enemies and kindly to my friends. For it is such people who live in the highest esteem.' This is the kind of language with which she exults in her success over Aegeus: 'now I shall win the victory over my enemies' (764–7), language that recalls the end of the scene with Creon with its image of the heroic Medea facing the 'test of courage'. These are all words that belong to the traditional code, in which the laughter of enemies is the ultimate disgrace and harming enemies and helping friends is the duty of a hero. But Medea's appropriation of the code seems hideously out of place in a situation where the enemy is her husband and the means of punishing him is to be an act of bloodthirsty treachery followed by the murder of her own children.

The essential relevance of the scene with Aegeus must be its stress on the value and importance of children. Euripides does not make clear exactly when Medea arrives at the details of her plan, and we cannot say that the encounter with Aegeus gives her the idea to kill the children; it is enough that after the scene with Aegeus she has the idea very fully worked out: this will be Jason's consummate punishment, to be robbed of his future. Her announcement comes as a surprise, but it is not factitious: the prologue's prophetic warnings and the prominence of the theme of parents and children in all three of Medea's encounters have effectively prepared the way.[2] This technique is perhaps subtler than the version preferred by Seneca, an episode in which Medea sees how much Jason loves his children and says 'Now I have him.'[3] Euripides' Medea does not need to be shown evidence of Jason's fatherly love: she simply knows that even a man as selfish and coarse-grained as Jason, who for the moment is quite absorbed in his young bride and his new social status and content for his whole family to go into exile, can still be profoundly hurt by the loss of his children.

Even more than the scene with Aegeus it is the child murder itself that has caused the greatest critical unease. Perhaps this is because society so much abhors the murder of children that it refuses to regard it as anything but the rarest and most outrageous of deviations. Hence the attempt to explain Medea's act as something quite outside the experience of civilized people. In general we tend not to look on murder as such with the same disbelief; and it comes as a surprise to find from modern statistics that a large proportion of murder victims are in fact children—nearly one-third of the total in the United Kingdom between 1957 and 1968,[4] nearly half in Denmark

2. Cf. D. Ebener, *Rheinisches Museum* 104 (1961), 224.
3. *Medea* 549–50: 'sic natos amat? | bene est, tenetur, uulneri patet locus' ['Does he love his children so much? / Good! Now I have him: there is a way to hurt him'].
4. Cf. E. Gibson and S. Klein, *Murder 1957 to 1968 = Home Office Research Studies* 3 (London 1969). I am grateful to my colleague Mrs A. M. Morris for a criminologist's view of the problem of child murder.

in recent times[5]—and that the killers are predominantly their parents. Often the killing of children is accompanied by suicide on the part of the parents, but one parent may kill a child or children as a means of hurting the marriage partner. May it not be that in *Medea* we find Euripides exhibiting the same psychological sureness of touch as in his studies of Phaedra and Electra and Pentheus, or as in the scene [in *Bacchae*] where Cadmus brings Agave back to reality?[6]

Medea is trying to achieve the punishment of Jason; the death of the princess and Creon is not enough, because through her children Medea can still be hurt or insulted (by the 'laughter of her enemies'), if *they* are hurt or insulted. With them alive and in his care Jason can still look to the future through them. There is no question of Medea's admitting to a wish to punish the children: she calls them 'most beloved' (795) and her deed 'most unholy' (796): only in the prologue does she curse them and the Nurse say she 'hates the children' (presumably because they represent her vulnerability to Jason). Indeed she thinks she is being loyal to her dear ones and winning glory by her actions (809f.), heroic language which a psychologist would probably describe as an 'altruistic' and 'protective' rationalization of the child murder. It seems that very often the parents who kill their children convince themselves that the children would in their own interests be better dead.[7]

The scene of false reconciliation between Medea and Jason makes magnificent theatre; it also has a subtle importance in its relation to the rest of the play.[8] It emphasizes the link between the two stages of Medea's revenge by showing the children who are to be victims of the culminating deed innocently bearing the poisoned gifts which will make them the agents of the first murder, with Jason as their accomplice. From 894ff. the children are the focus of the action; and seeing them in Jason's embraces and hearing his confident words about their future, Medea twice breaks down, though each time she resourcefully contrives to explain her tears in a sense which furthers her deception of Jason. The episode has a complex function: it confirms our awareness of the children's importance to Jason and at the same time prepares for the moving passage (1029ff.) where Medea imagines the future that the children will never have. Moreover her self-mastery here, according to Steidle's persuasive analysis,[9] foreshadows the success of her resolve in the following scene. Certainly it must now seem clear to the audience, as it does to the chorus, that the children are bound to die: 'Now no longer have I any hope

5. Cf. T. Harder, *Acta Psychiatrica Scandinavica* 43 (1967), 197ff.
6. Cf. G. Devereux, *J.H.S.* 90 (1970), 35ff. for a study of this scene.
7. Harder (n. 5 above), pp. 235ff.
8. Cf. A. Lesky, *Die tragische Dichtung der Hellenen*, 3rd ed. (Göttingen 1972), p. 307; Steidle, *Studien*, pp. 156f.
9. See n. 8 above.

left for the children's lives, no longer. They go already to their deaths'
(976ff.).

Now Medea learns that the first part of her plan has worked and
the children have been allowed to stay in Corinth; she must say good-
bye to them, ostensibly because she is going into exile, but we know
that she confronts the essential issue. Time is short, and without the
death of the children her revenge will not be complete; but can she
face the deed? The speech at 1021ff. in which she expresses the struggle between her maternal love and her desire for revenge has been
tirelessly discussed:[1] is it the tragic climax of the play, showing Medea
caught in a conflict on the outcome of which we hang in suspense, or
is the inevitability that she will kill her children strongly felt all
through the speech, and the climax reached only in the final scene?
Recent critics have been particularly concerned with the structural
question and also with the apparent inconsistency of Medea's motivation. Within the space of a few lines she moves from the statement
that she will take the children with her into exile (1058) to the asser-
tion that there is no escape: they are certain to be killed in Corinth,
and she must therefore do the deed (1059–64).

The detail of the speech suggests that despite a certain rhetorical
formalism of manner Euripides keeps close to observed patterns of
human behaviour. The reality of Medea's love for her children is
evoked in her very precise recall of the hopes she used to cherish for
their future and hers (1024–35) and in her response to the extraordinarily powerful appeal of their bright eyes and soft skin (1070–5).
But the reality of her obsessive need to triumph over her enemies is
also made inescapably clear (1049–55; 1059–60), the need to hurt
Jason as deeply as anyone can ever be hurt, which has been fully
explored earlier in the play, both in the betrayed wife's passion for
vengeance and in the heroic self-image which makes Medea a far
from ordinary but none the less convincing and tragic figure.

Euripides needs to make us believe in Medea's maternal feeling not
because we are to think there is a real hope that she may change her
mind for good, but in order to achieve the full depth of tragic serious-
ness. The deed she contemplates is so horrific that we cannot accept
it unless we are given evidence that it has cost a profound struggle.
Comparison with Seneca illustrates very well the difference between
tragic and melodramatic treatment of the situation. Seneca's Medea
carries conviction only as a raving madwoman, whose moments of
maternal feeling (938ff.) show none of the Euripidean Medea's precise awareness of what children mean to a mother. In any case, her
softer emotions soon give way to visions of Furies accompanying the
dismembered Apsyrtus, to whom Medea sacrifices one of the children,

1. Cf. A. Lesky (n. 8 above), pp. 311f.

keeping the other to be killed in full view of Jason and the citizens. With her intended victim at her side she expresses a fleeting sense of remorse, but this is soon lost in the joy of gloating over Jason; of the child's presumed agony she seems (like Seneca) to be unaware:

> quid, misera, feci? misera? paeniteat licet,
> feci. uoluptas magna me inuitam subit,
> et ecce crescit. derat hoc unum mihi,
> spectator iste.   (990–3)

> [What, unhappy wretch, have I done? Unhappy?
>   Even if I regret it,
> I have done it. A great pleasure comes over me
>   against my will,
> and look! it grows! Only this one thing was missing,
> for Jason to be watching.]

Euripides' master-stroke in this speech is Medea's announcement at 1059ff. that there is no going back: the poison must have done its work by now and the princess must already be dead. We can assume that the treacherous murder of the princess and Creon will in reality mean danger for the children from the outraged royal family (as Jason later confirms, 1303ff.). Medea's reaction, when she faces the fact that the murder must have happened, is to treat this danger as inescapable, although a moment earlier she has been speaking of taking the children away with her. She is filled, in fact, with a sudden sense that she is caught in the tide of events and has no longer any choice. This is the atmosphere of sudden urgency in which we are told that the murder of children is often committed: the parent becomes convinced of a threat to the children that clinches the feeling that they would be better dead.[2] Such an interpretation seems much more relevant to Medea's case than any of the others that have been put forward, of which the latest is that the children were too young to accompany their mother in a hasty escape.[3]

The sense of urgency is brought to a desperate climax in Medea's speech after the Messenger has told his story and urged her to fly. There is no word now of triumph over her enemies or of her own situation at all beyond her need to steel herself: her whole concentration is on the children. She must act 'as swiftly as possible', 'without delay'; since they are bound to be killed, she who loves them must be the one to do the deed, not some 'other more hostile hand' (1239ff.). The murder itself is represented by means of cries from

---

2. Cf. Harder (n. 5 above), especially p. 237, and L. Bender, *Journal of Nervous and Mental Disease* 80 (1934), 41.
3. Steidle (n. 6 above), pp. 159ff.

the children and the chorus, but without any word from Medea; nowhere is there any hint of the gloating of Seneca's Medea as she raises the knife: 'perfruere lento scelere, ne propera, dolor' ['o bitter heart, don't rush, enjoy a leisurely crime'] (1016).

The gloating (but never over the children) is to come in the stark final scene where Medea triumphs over Jason from the chariot, prophesying an evil death for him, refusing to let him even touch the children's bodies. The brute fact of Jason's loss moves us now; but it is Medea who speaks with prophetic authority. Clearly she has the role of the 'god from the machine' who so often in Euripides makes the final dispositions. This is one of the most alarming features of the play, the fact that there is no comparatively distant and objective divine figure to speak with the voice of authority, relating these events to real life through their link with some cult or institution and thereby restoring a sense of normality after the frightful extremes of the action. Medea makes a link between this story and a festival at Corinth (1381ff.); but she offers no relief whatever from the horror of the situation.

The powerful effect of this final scene depends on Euripides' use of the supernatural device of the dragon chariot, which transforms Medea's status from that of runaway criminal to something outside ordinary human experience. It was a bold dramatic experiment, but Euripides was justified in making it, granted that the effect could be adequately and not absurdly represented on the Greek stage. There has been criticism of the contrast between this very blatant use of the supernatural and the realistic tone of the rest of the action,[4] but some kind of miraculous device was needed if Euripides was to contrive a final confrontation between Jason and Medea in which Medea should at last have her triumph. The whole plot in fact rests on unrealistic data which we accept without qualm: for example, Medea's relationship to Helios [the Sun] (a frequently stressed motif which helps to prepare for the chariot) and the remarkable nature of her magical power. Yet throughout we are invited to take Medea seriously as a real human being, and even this final scene is perfectly consistent with the rest of the play in its handling of her motivation; it is only the spectacle of her in the chariot, high above Jason, taking with her the children's bodies that he may not touch, that makes her seem to have been transformed, in Murray's words, 'into a sort of living Curse. . . . Her wrongs and her hate fill the sky'.[5]

The sense that Euripides seems to be making out of all this is as comfortless as the conclusions to which he points in *Hippolytus* or

4. R. Lattimore, for instance, regards the chariot as 'preposterous', merely a 'taxi to get from Corinth to Athens' (*The Poetry of Greek Tragedy* (Baltimore 1958), p. 108).
5. Murray (n. 2 above), pp. xif.

Bacchae. What a vulnerable thing is civilization, when man's passions are so powerfully destructive. When he makes the insensitive Jason praise Greek society and values and when he gives the barbarian witch the ideals of a traditional Greek hero he is surely suggesting that there is no safe dividing line: civilized life is always most pre-cariously poised, continually threatened from within.

One of the play's recurrent themes is that of song and the Muses: it comes in that curious passage at the end of the *parodos* where the Nurse meditatively wonders why poets have not devised songs to cure human miseries instead of accompanying their pleasures (190ff.); in the first *stasimon* when the chorus reflect how poetry has always represented the man's side of things (421ff.); most promi-nently in the great passage in praise of Athens after the departure of Aegeus (824ff.). Athens, city of the Muses, the ideal of civilized splendour, where *Sophia* and the Loves are in harmony: is this merely a fine compliment to an Athenian audience, or is it related more intimately to the deeper meaning of the play? All these pas-sages draw attention to the ambivalence of human intelligence and creativity, which is potentially a source of beauty and harmony, but liable, too, to break out in destructive violence under the influence of passion. Medea in her *sophia* exemplifies this ambivalence: we see her great expertise and intellectual power turned, because of her betrayed love for Jason, to destructive—and self-destructive—ends. And her heroic sense of identity is used to bring out the tragic nature of what she does and suffers.

HELENE P. FOLEY

From Medea's Divided Self[†]

Like Clytemnestra in the absence of her husband Agamemnon, Euripides' Medea becomes in essence a woman without a *kurios* or guardian. She has irrevocably severed bonds with her natal family and her homeland, her husband Jason has married the Corinthian princess and deserted his family, and finally, she faces imminent exile from Corinth. Yet despite her apparent helplessness, Medea has no effective opponents in this play but herself. The play becomes a laboratory in which the audience can observe a mature woman attempt to make and carry out a critical decision about avenging her wrongs in a context where her husband refuses to treat her as a ratio-nal peer or to recognize her grievances against him. This choice is

† From *Female Acts in Greek Tragedy* (Princeton: Princeton UP, 2001), pp. 243–44, 257–68. Reprinted by permission of Princeton University Press.

made both outside the confines of either the natal or marital households that normally define the space in which a woman lives, and outside the confines of a city in which she is in any sense a citizen.[1] A normal Greek woman had accessible no model of full social and ethical autonomy available to herself. The decision to avenge her wrongs presents no problems for Medea; she borrows heroic masculine ethical standards to articulate her choice and stereotypically feminine duplicity and magic permit her to achieve her goals. In effecting her revenge, her major problem is at first how to carry out her plans given the tools available to her. Yet this revenge comes to seem in her view to require the killing of her own children.

Although eloquent about the wrongs marriage and society inflict on women, Medea struggles to find an ethical voice that can articulate her maternal concerns and her female self-interest, despite her husband's view that she has no serious cultural need for her children, because the boys were born (at least originally) to reproduce the paternal line and are supported by their father (565, 460–62). Aeschylus' Clytemnestra claimed ownership of her daughter Iphigeneia; Medea seems finally able only to achieve her goals by disowning her sons and the maternal commitment that blocks her autonomy, thus accepting the permanent suffering that she inflicts on herself. This essay examines closely the implications of Medea's self-division in the context of the gender relations developed in the play as a whole.

✳   ✳   ✳

Gender and Self-Division

Through a careful dramatic orchestration of the relation between the two engendered sides of Medea that is echoed in the conflict between male and female characters,[2] the earlier scenes of *Medea* prepare for the climactic display of self-division in the monologue. (By contrast, the play does not prepare the audience to confront in the monologue a conflict between passion and reason or between two emotions.) The first scene provides disturbing hints about the contradictory aspects of Medea's character. On the one hand, Medea seems suicidal, a helpless, feminine victim of her husband's desertion. She has sacrificed everything for Jason. This is the side of Medea that moves and impresses the chorus of women. On the other hand, the nurse, as she expresses her fears about the dangerous

---

1. Friedrich 1993 stresses Medea's lack of grounding in the ethics of *oikos* [household] and *polis* [city], and Rabinowitz 1993: 128 and 138 her dangerous independence of male protection and supervision.
2. See Schlesinger's emphasis (1966: 45) on the pervasive conflict between male and female worlds in the play and Williamson 1985 (rev. 1990) on gender and space.

temperament of the proud and wrathful heroine, anticipates in her language Medea's own heroic view of herself. Her nature is royal (119–21; see Medea at 403–6); she is self-willed (*authadous,* 104; see Medea at 1028), high-spirited, and hard to check (*megalosplanchnos* and *duskatapaustos,* 109) and, in her anger against the injustice (26) and dishonor (20, 33) done to her, may turn against her own *philoi* [friends and family] (95). From the moment of her first appearance on stage, Medea's female side is in this play not taken for granted but carefully defined through the relationship she creates with the chorus.[3] Her heroic, masculine side only emerges explicitly in the speeches (364–409, 764–810) where Medea announces her revenge plans, although it is implied to a lesser degree in her first and final forthright encounters with Jason.

At her first entrance Medea makes an appeal to the chorus as fellow married women by describing her own situation in terms of the difficult life of all women and their potential for becoming victims of a male order (230–51). With this speech Medea obtains the silence of the chorus and—surprisingly, given her myth—establishes a strong association between herself and the ordinary housewife in a Greek city. The women of the chorus approve her revenge on Jason (267) and even tacitly consent to the destruction of members of their own royal family, although they do not wish to be tortured by *erōs* like Medea but desire for themselves a moderate Aphrodite appropriate to a proper wife (635–41). For them, Medea's eloquence and just complaints against Jason and Creon represent a reversal of poetry's silencing of women through the centuries and its maligning of them as sexually unfaithful (410–30). The women of the chorus only break with Medea, see her as other than themselves and unlike women, when she determines to include the killing of the children in her revenge on Jason. The protection of children from harm is such an intimate part of the self-interest of mothers (the women repeatedly remind Medea of the negative effects that the crime will have on herself: see esp. 818, 996–97, and 1261 on the waste of Medea's efforts in rearing her children), that they can think of only one example of a woman who killed her children, Ino, and she (unlike Medea) was mad when she committed her crime and followed the murder by suicide (1282–89).[4]

3. There seem to be two reasons for this. First, the play can win sympathy for Medea as victimized woman before revealing the full range of her differences from her own sex; second, Euripides must confront the mythological tradition, which often envisioned Medea as a witch with magic powers. See, however, Knox 1977: 204 and 212–13 for the ways that Euripides plays down Medea's supernatural powers here, at least until the concluding scene. Rohdich 1968: 47–55 overemphasizes the degree to which Medea has become merely a woman in this play. Barlow's 1989 argument has some similarities to my own.

4. As Visser 1986: 158 points out, women kill their children in Greek myth elsewhere only to avenge their kin.

The case for Medea as an ill-treated female victim is tellingly built up in the early scenes of the play where she adopts traditionally "feminine" weapons in her self-defense. Both Creon's gesture of immediate exile for a woman who has nowhere to go and Jason's indifference to it seem extraordinarily callous, as the shocked reaction of King Aegeus to Medea's plight later confirms (704–7; see also the nurse at 82–84 and the chorus at 576–78). The egotistical Jason has clearly given little thought to his family's welfare, despite his belated protests to the contrary, and his callous behavior in his first scene with Medea cannot but call attention to her beleaguered situation. Creon is aware of Medea's unusual intelligence and her capacity for anger, but Medea deceives him into a temporary reprieve by using the weapons of the weak: supplication (338) and an appeal to her children's welfare (340–47). Medea also gives up trying to persuade Jason honestly. Instead, she successfully feigns being the helpless woman, given to tears and irrationality, who will now for the good of her children accept, as a proper woman should, her husband's superiority and guidance. This feminine role playing, which in the second scene with Jason does have some basis in Medea's feeling for the children, dupes even her own husband, who should (like the nurse) have known better.

These early scenes of the play, by building a powerful case for male exploitation of women and Medea's entrapment in a female role, may temporarily distract the audience from the initial contradictory view of a dangerous Medea presented above all by the nurse in the first scene. Increasingly, however, the text emphasizes Medea's distance from her carefully contrived appearance of solidarity with her fellow women, as she uses her "femininity," the desire for children, and even her own maternal love to manipulate and deceive not only Creon and Jason but even her supporter Aegeus. Furthermore, as several critics have pointed out, her eloquent first speech on the wrongs of women deceptively applies only in part to herself.[5] For Medea is far from the passive victim of marriage and masculine brutality that she claims to be. Unlike the typical housewife, she did not in fact need the dowry she complains of to the chorus (232–34); she chose her own husband and has won him by her ruthless deeds. Indeed, she often seems to envision herself, contrary to Greek practice, as an equal or even the dominant partner in the marriage. Note Medea's use of the feminine active participle *gamousa*, at 606 (women normally marry in the middle, not the active voice); she speaks of her gift to the princess as *phernas*, or dowry (956). In her view the choice of a husband is an *agōn*, a contest (235). The clasping of right hands that confirmed Medea's marriage to Jason is a

5. See esp. Pucci 1980: 64–69, Bongie 1977: 36, and Easterling 1977: 182.

gesture typical of the affirmation of bonds between men;[6] in the standard marriage the man grasps the woman's wrist in a gesture of domination. Medea speaks of reconciliation with Jason as if it were a truce between two cities (898).

Extraordinarily intelligent (*sophē*), Medea can sing an answer to the other sex (426–27). She is not, as the chorus continues to believe (1290–92), motivated only by betrayal in bed (265–66). Medea is also responsible for Jason's fame (476–82; she even, probably contrary to the better-known tradition, kills the dragon herself, 480–82), as he himself indirectly admits when he says that she should be consoled for what has happened to her because if she had not come to Greece *she* would not have been famous (see 536–41). Medea would prefer battle to childbirth (250–51), and Euripides uses the language of athletic contest to describe her struggles against Jason (44–45, 765, 366–67, 403, 1245). Despite her own denial (407–9), Medea, though a woman, has the capacity actively to do good, as the Corinthians and Aegeus know.[7] We are told by the nurse that Medea won the favor of the Corinthians (11–12, probably by averting a famine [see the scholiast at Pindar *Olympian* 13.74; in some versions of her myth, Medea even ruled Corinth for a while]);[8] she wins a promise from King Aegeus that because she can make him fertile, she may live under his protection in Athens.

The desire to avenge erotic betrayal is characteristic of women in Greek poetry, as we see from the chorus's sympathetic reaction to Medea and from Medea's own words (263–66; see also Jason at 909–10); so is Medea's choice of weapon, poison, and the deceptive rhetoric and gestures (tears, suppliancy) with which she manipulates her masculine enemies. Yet the side of Medea that plans and executes revenge, and especially the death of the children, is not represented in the language of the play as "feminine."[9] Above all, as Knox and Bongie in particular point out, the avenging Medea thinks and acts not like a classical woman but like an archaic and Sophoclean hero when he feels he has been wronged. Her first offstage words, her screams of suicidal rage, which threaten to endanger even those she loves, may be deliberately reminiscent of Sophocles' Ajax.[1] Her brilliance, craft, and drive for survival recall the Homeric Odysseus. Like Ajax or Achilles, she would deliberately sacrifice friends

---

6. Flory 1978: 70–71.
7. Easterling 1977: 179 emphasizes that Aegeus treats Medea as a respectable religious authority.
8. See the scholiast at *Medea* 9 and 264.
9. As was emphasized earlier, when Medea describes her plans she stresses the rational and heroic motivations for her revenge and virtually ignores the erotic ones.
1. See Knox 1977: 96. Friedrich 1993: 223 argues that Medea does not represent a genuine example of heroic ethos because she flatters, lies, abases herself. Nevertheless, Medea does adopt an heroic ethos, even if her actions in some respects betray it.

to defend her honor against a public slight from a peer. She has the stubborn individualism, intransigence, power, near-bestial savagery, and lack of pity of such beleaguered heroes. As hero, she wants to do good to her friends and bad to her enemies, quell injustice, win fame (810), and protect her reputation. She is so fearless that the sword would be her weapon of choice if circumstances permitted its use (379–85, 393). Poison, the feminine weapon, is her choice of necessity (ironically, she goes back to the sword to kill her helpless children). No woman in tragedy—none of all those who take revenge—models her self-image so explicitly on a masculine heroic and even military model (see esp. 1242–45).[2] Like a hero, she wishes to live up to her identity as the child of noble ancestors; she is the granddaughter of the sun: "Advance into danger. Now is your trial of courage. You see what you suffer. You must not be mocked by Jason's Sisyphean marriage, for you are descended from a noble father and the sun" (403–6).

What is shocking about Medea, as opposed, for example, to Clytemnestra in *Agamemnon*, where we are told from the first of her masculine aspects, is that Medea's heroic side emerges fully only as the play goes on, as she shrugs off the mask of subservience she has accepted as Jason's wife and finds the means to effect her revenge.[3] I have argued that the audience, like the chorus, is at first partly deceived by Medea's view of her plight as typically female. The first scene hints at Medea's outrage and capacity for violence, but those hints are obscured by her threats of suicide, her domestic confinement, her solidarity with the chorus, and her use of "feminine" wiles to manipulate Creon, Jason, and even Aegeus. Euripides' audience probably did not know that Medea would deliberately destroy her children or escape in the sun's chariot at the end.[4] It may even

---

2. See Bongie 1977: 28 and 30–31 on Medea's masculinity, in contrast to Knox 1977, who sees Medea as heroic on the Sophoclean model regardless of sex. When they speak and act as Attic women could not or should not, many tragic heroines, and especially Sophoclean heroines, are characterized by the text as masculine. Medea's behavior is set apart from that of any other "masculine" tragic heroine above all by the language in which she describes her revenge. Even Clytemnestra, with her man-counseling (*Agamemnon* 11) mind, describes her killing of her husband in *Agamemnon* not with military metaphors but with language that perverts ritual and cycles of nature. Hecuba in Euripides' *Hecuba*, whose situation and revenge are very similar to Medea's, lacks her sense of heroic dignity at all costs. She says that she would accept slavery in exchange for the chance to obtain revenge (756–57).
3. Gellie 1988: esp. 16 laments the lack of psychological coherence in the portrait of Medea. "All these Medeas cannot fail to get in each others' way." This is arguable, but at least in this play the generation of contradictory aspects in the character seems consistent and deliberate. On the question of continuity in Greek, and especially Euripidean (Gould 1978: 51–52) characterization, see further the introduction to this book.
4. Even if Neophron's version of the play, in which Medea chooses to kill the children herself, came first (Manuwald 1983 and Michelini 1989), the audience would not be certain whether Euripides' Medea would do so, or whether, as in other versions of the myth, the Corinthians killed them. See Page [1938] 1971: xxi–xxv, Buttrey 1958:13–14, and McDermott 1989: 25–42.

have feared for some time, as T. Buttrey argues,[5] that Medea was unwittingly destroying herself by leading her children into a death trap.

Medea plays for Creon, Aegeus, and finally Jason the part of the tragic damsel in distress in need of a masculine rescue, which she finally acquires in part from Aegeus.[6] But as the feminine mask gradually slips to reveal first an archaic hero and finally a near-goddess, the story of her revenge takes on a pattern typical of divine rather than human action.[7] Dionysus in Euripides' *Bacchae*, for example, punishes disbelievers who fail to revere him and to penetrate his disguise. Similarly, the once victimized and seemingly powerless Medea appears finally as a semidivine Fury whose nature and authority were not recognized by the mortals around her (except, to some degree, the nurse). While fully aware of Medea's intelligence, Creon (286), Jason (527–28, 555, 568–73, 1338), and even the chorus (1291–92) see Medea as a woman, and therefore as motivated only by jealousy (whereas she herself mentions this motive only at 265–66, 1354, and 1368 and in each case more is at stake in her anger over her bed than sexual jealousy). For Jason, Medea is a temperamental barbarian concubine (and a typical woman) who must be cast aside for the advantages of a real Greek marriage. Jason mistakenly fails to treat Medea as a hero, to value their mutual oaths and her favors to himself. He cannot hear the heroic language and values she adopts for herself in their first encounter.[8] And so, like Pentheus, he pays for his misunderstanding.

But before the final revelation of her superhumanity, Medea has been shown to have a masculine and a feminine side, each exercising its capacity for reason and emotion. The two sides at first establish an uneasy complicity in the pursuit of revenge but finally split in tragic conflict during the famous monologue, By the conclusion of the monologue Medea's female self is once more a victim, this time both of her masculine self and of Jason, for at 1074 (see also 1364 and 1397–98) she blames her husband for the children's death (presumably because she cannot succeed in punishing him without

5. Buttrey 1958: 12. Ohlander 1989 expands considerably on his approach.
6. Gredley 1987: 30–32 notes Medea's consistent control of her performance and her transformation of a position of ritualized inferiority—suppliancy—into one of dominance. Boedeker 1991: 106–9 stresses the way that she authors, rehearses, and directs her own story.
7. This shift from a rescue to a revenge plot-pattern is implied in Buttrey's discussion of the structure of the play (1958: 10; see also Burnett 1973: 8). Burnett argues that the messenger speech describes the death of the princess in an explicit fashion characteristic of divine revenge plays (17). Many critics have noticed the similarities between the conclusion of *Bacchae* and *Medea*. On Medea as dea ex machina, see esp. Cunningham 1954: 152, Collinge 1962: 170–72, Knox 1977: 206–11, Worthington 1990, and Ohander 1989: 189, who emphasizes Medea's human side in this final appearance.
8. See Bongie 1977: 42; see Gill 1996 on Jason's general failure to comprehend Medea and her positions.

killing the children). What is Euripides' point in turning the tragedy of jealousy that we expect in the first scene into a tragedy of
gender? By this I mean, not that Medea's tragedy is *about* gender,
but that it raises its tragic issues as a double conflict between male
and female, both on stage in the external world and within Medea's
self. And what is the significance of the structure of the play, in
which the hero and finally the divinity in Medea emerge to dominate, if not entirely obscure, the victimized woman?[9]

Euripides' plays tend to leave us, as here, with more questions and
(possible) revolutionary critiques than answers. The attitude of the
chorus of ordinary women reminds us that for Euripides' audience a
proper Greek wife had no fully autonomous sense of self, no muse, no
public voice (421–30, 1085–89). As we have seen, legally she was
under the permanent supervision of a guardian and could make no
significant decisions. Any independent action on the part of a classical Athenian woman, or any pursuit of her own desires, was not
acceptable in a wife unless it involved carrying out household duties
such as weaving, cooking, or guarding and caring for household property and children (see also the *Odyssey's* Penelope, who takes action
only in these matters). Nor did a woman, living confined to the
household and religious activities, have the knowledge or the educated discipline needed to make independent decisions (see, e.g.,
Sophocles' Deianeira in *Women of Trachis*). Tragic heroes like Medea
frequently do not play by the rules governing the conduct of Attic
women, yet these limits are, I think, implicitly present in the language
and structure of all tragedies.[1] For every action a tragic woman takes
in her own interest—every action outside of self-sacrifice for family or
community—receives explicit criticism within the plays as unfeminine and has destructive consequences. Even Antigone is condemned
for her unfeminine behavior and brings two other deaths in her wake.

Is Euripides' *Medea*, then, confirming the audience's worst fears
of what will happen when a woman takes action?[2] Is it anticipating
Aristotle in arguing that women are naturally *akuros*, without autonomous moral authority,[3] that because they cannot control their

---

9. My previous discussion does not intend to question the reality of Medea's female and
   victimized self; she remains, despite her rhetoric, confined within female social limits
   until her final supernatural departure. Her use of the magical poison (see Knox 1977:
   214) does not by itself characterize her as a witch. A similar poison, a typical female
   weapon, is used (unintentionally) by the feminine Deianeira of Sophocles. As Segal
   1996: 28 puts it, her ethos may be masculine, but her crime is feminine.
1. See esp. Loraux 1987, Harder 1993, and Seidensticker 1995.
2. Rabinowitz 1993: 125–27, 149–50 takes this view (see also McDermott 1989: 50 and
   64). She argues that the victimized Medea loses the audience's sympathy through her
   crimes and affirms its fears that women may escape the nets of male domination and
   become threats to male children. Female subjectivity is dangerous, especially if they
   are willing to harm themselves to gain revenge.
3. Implied in Fortenbaugh's discussion at 1970: 238–39. As was remarked before, Jason
   repeatedly sees Medea's only motive for action as *erōs*. Medea flatteringly distracts Jason
   from his view of female nature by pretending to imitate him.

emotions with reason they cannot be permitted moral independence but must, as Jason thinks Medea should, obey the plans of their more reasonable husbands (see 565–75)? And all the more so because women are so clever at the rational planning of ways to achieve the goals dictated by their emotions (see esp. 407–9 and Creon's fear of Medea's intelligence)? These are in fact the very cultural clichés that Medea exploits in her second scene with Jason, where she pretends to accept and conform to his notions of what a woman is like and what she should be. In her speech at 869–905, Medea plays on women's supposed inferiority to men in making judgments (889–93) and emphasizes the wisdom of obeying those planning wisely for herself, the king and her husband, and the folly of her anger (873–78, 882–83, 885, 892–93). Later in the scene she hides the true reason for her tears at the sight of the children by remarking that women are given to tears (928).

Although Greek tragedy generally tends by displaying the devastating consequences of inverting cultural norms ultimately to affirm those norms, our earlier discussion of the monologue has made it clear that this interpretation of *Medea* cannot be true in any simple sense. For we must not forget that Euripides has presented in a negative light and even punished the ethical behavior of all the male characters in the play except Aegeus,[4] who sides with Medea and displays a heroic integrity comparable with the heroine's, and that the vengeful Medea deliberately imitates a heroic brand of masculinity. Because there is for the Greeks no model of autonomous and heroic femininity outside of self-sacrifice, Medea can only turn to a male model if she wishes to act authoritatively and with *timē* (honor). If she acts in a way that guarantees self-preservation and child preservation, she will in male public terms lose face and fail to make a dramatic display of her wrongs. Like all disfranchised rebels, she can tragically imagine no other self or self-defense to imitate than that of her oppressors. By this I mean, not that she sets out to imitate Jason or Creon, but that the heroic code itself oppresses women, both because it traditionally excludes and subordinates them and because it gives priority to public success and honor over survival and the private concerns of love and family. The debate between Hector and Andromache in *Iliad* 6, in which the views of the proper wife lose out to those of the warrior responsible to the welfare of his people, makes this clear in a more benign way. In this play we see that oppression in the inability of Jason to recognize Medea's heroic self and in Medea's own failure to accept the arguments of her

---

4. See Schlesinger 1966: 45. Burnett argues that this atmosphere of moral corruption makes tragic Medea's otherwise monstrous and archaic revenge.

maternal voice.[5] Furthermore, as G. B. Walsh and Pietro Pucci have shown, the Medea who contests Jason's injustice and pursuit of profit at the cost of emotional pain (598–99) ends up adopting all too similar goals for herself.[6] She chooses to accept emotional pain in order to achieve her revenge; a victim of injustice, she ends up like Jason, wronging her friends and rejecting suppliants (the chorus who pleads for the children at 853–55, and, by implication, the children, 863).[7] She wants to be understood and accepted for what she is (215–24; 292–305), but ends by doing everything to hide what she is from those around her. Thus, by pursuing her heroic code she ends by imitating even her despised immediate oppressors and harming herself.

For a moment in the monologue we may hope that her maternal side will successfully contest the masculine heroic logic, but everything in Medea and her circumstances has conspired against this frail possibility. For Medea has tried to suppress this voice too long. In addition, she has come to envision all that is female as despicable,[8] a source of oppression that denies her need to be accepted for her own capacities and to achieve due recognition, a source of bad and never of good (407–9). For Medea, women are cowards except when they are wronged in bed (263–66); they are forced to depend on one person (247); they must buy a master for their bodies (232–34); any reputation they have must be to their disadvantage (215–24, 292–93). Maternity and *erōs*—emotional dependence on others—have tied her to Jason and led her to the predicament in which she is now trapped. In the monologue the maternal voice appears to her masculine self to present only the "soft arguments" of a cowardice to be expected from women (1052; see also 1242–46 and 776). Finally, Medea's repeated use of her femininity to manipulate and deceive has reduced her

---

5. Rehm 1989 independently offered a discussion along these lines. I differ from him largely in thinking that the female voice that opposes the heroic masculine logic in Medea is less articulated in the play and far more fragile. Ohlander 1989: 144 argues that Medea's desire to kill the children rather than allow the Corinthians to do so arises from her need to enlist her mother love in the cause of her revenge.

6. See the very different arguments of Walsh 1979: 296–99 and Pucci 1980: esp. chs. 2 and 4, who emphasizes how the oppressed Medea adopts the position of a master. Strohm 1957: 3 shows how the positions of Jason and Medea have been precisely reversed by the exodus (for linguistic echoes of the earlier scene in the later one, see Burnett 1973: 22). The same is true for prologue and exodus. Jason begins by devaluing children for expedient reasons and ends as movingly paternal. Medea, in her movement toward masculinity, follows the reverse course.

7. At 1250 Medea, just before killing the children, admits they were *philoi*: but it is too late to recognize the full irony of her position. Schein 1990 now elaborates on these points and Boedeker 1991 stresses the contemporary political resonance of Jason's perversion of oaths, supplication, and persuasion.

8. On the general point, see Pucci 1980: 64. Jason, Creon, and even the chorus make other negative judgments of women. Galis 1992: esp. 77 sees Medea as betrayed by the very womanhood and reproductive capacity that she comes to hate.

womanly side to a role so lacking in heroic integrity that she can only wish to slough it off.

Moreover, through the chorus, we have already seen how the female voice, silenced for centuries, lacks the confidence and authority necessary to make a reply to a long masculine tradition. The women of the chorus hoped to find this female voice in Medea, after her brilliant exposure of marriage and Jason's betrayal; but even they did not really expect a victimized woman to live up to their hopes (410–45). Later, aware after the monologue that they have lost their spokeswoman[9]—or, in fact, that they had never had one—the previously timid women struggle to give voice to the female muse in themselves and fail (1081–1115). Pitifully, their reasoning leads them to lose their grip on their one certainty, their commitment to maternity and the preservation of the lives of the children, as they wonder if it would not be better never to experience parenthood at all.[1] If the women of the chorus can be swayed momentarily to abandon the core of their self-interest as women, it is hardly surprising that the brilliant and semidivine princess Medea finds in her maternity no positive basis for action.[2]

Is Euripides, then, making in *Medea* a tragic point about social oppression and social change? Medea has been treated unjustly by men, and her eloquent indictment of women's lot is never denied.[3] By developing the case for Medea's oppression first, the play seems to urge us to understand Medea's later behavior as a reaction to this oppression. We saw in the monologue how Medea's female side predictably (especially given the gender relations obtaining in Greek culture) fell victim to her masculine side and Jason. Jason's failure to treat Medea as the fully human (rather than, in a traditional Greek sense, female) and even heroic being he married with a clasp of right hands and supplicated in times of trouble propels her to ever greater daring. His own significant—if not, as Medea sometimes claims, exclusive—responsibility for the tragic outcome seems confirmed both by the appearance of the sun's chariot and by the plot pattern that structures the final scenes. Reckford sees in the alienation and

---

9. The third and fourth stasima [choral odes] reverse the chorus' earlier hopes and reveal its despair and horror at Medea.

1. As Wolff 1982: 240 notes, by coming, like Medea, to overvalue self-sufficiency, the women deny the human need for reproduction. Reckford 1968: 346 sees in this chorus a divorce between reason and feeling.

2. We do not know that the chorus comprises married women, but it consistently champions Medea's maternal interests as critical to her female identity and welfare.

3. Even if, as Pucci 1980: 65–69 argues, Medea's argument contradicts itself, it presents a substantially accurate indictment of contemporary Attic reality. See Knox 1977: 219–21, Reckford 1968: 336–39, Paduano 1968: 259–71, and Barlow 1989 and 1995, who argues that Euripides' challenge to female stereotypes and the marriage system in the play survives the reemergence of popular misogyny at the conclusion.

corruption of Medea the self-fulfilling power of prejudice.[4] Yet Euripides also seems to imply that the oppressed, by being trapped into imitating their oppressors, can in the end only tragically silence what should have been their own true (here maternal) voice, destroy themselves, and confirm an unjust status quo.

Or is Euripides, as Wolff suggests, also using *Medea* to bring home a point about masculine ethics?[5] Greek poets repeatedly demonstrated the tragic consequences of the brand of heroic individualism imitated by Medea and of the "do good to friends, bad to enemies" ethic. Here Medea, like Achilles (or Ajax), destroys (or threatens to destroy) in her heroic wrath those who are her friends. She talks herself into believing that her revenge will be inadequate without the death of the children; for when the chorus asks her how she could endure to kill her own offspring, she replies that her husband would above all be tortured (*dēchtheiē*, 817; see also 1370) by this. Yet unlike Achilles, who regains a fuller humanity in *Iliad* 24, Medea finally leaves female and even human limits (including human ethical limits) behind. The audience is literally distanced from her as she appears high above the stage, and for the first time it is invited to feel pity for Jason, who, wracked with paternal anguish, has lost all identity with the loss of his children. By choosing Medea, a barbarian woman, to display the contradictions inherent in this heroic ethic and behavior, Euripides has achieved a particularly devastating and grotesque demonstration of the problematic (above all because self-destructive) nature of this archaic heroism—and one he might have hesitated to make through a Greek or male protagonist.[6]

True, there is a certain integrity in Medea's single-minded pursuit of this archaic masculine ethic, especially when we are offered as an alternative the dubious sophistic or unprincipled masculine behavior of Creon and Jason. The play uses Medea's heroic ethic to expose the callous amoral pragmatism of the unheroic Jason[7] and Creon, and then turns on the ethic itself as it deteriorates into a ghastly version of her enemies' behavior. By implicitly taking as her heroic models both the avenging archaic warrior Achilles and the clever and crafty survivor Odysseus, and thus conflating two brands of heroism that epic views as partially contradictory, Medea shows

---

4. Reckford 1968: 345. See also Reckford 346 n. 26 on the possible allusions in Medea's case to the plight of noncitizen wives in Athens after Pericles' citizenship law of 451/0. Knox 1977: 222 sees in the hostility expressed toward Medea as a *sophē* a reflection of Euripides' own reception by his contemporaries.

5. Wolf 1982: 238–39. Michelini 1989: 132 thinks that the play offers a critique of the heroic code's sacrifice of social obligation.

6. Burnett 1973 argued that Euripides stripped Medea's revenge of all the circumstances that mitigate other tragic revenges. Burnett 1998 now takes a more sympathetic view of the heroine's revenge; the crime is meant to produce not only horror and consternation, but pity for the seriously wronged heroine (194).

7. See von Fritz 1962: 322–429 on how the play deprives Jason of his epic heroism.

herself a pathetically confused imitator of heroic masculinity.[8] By adhering blindly to her warrior code, she ironically comes to the peak of daring (394): the slaughter of her own children.[9] She achieves not the fame she sought but infamy. By going beyond the tragic, by not paying for her revenge with suicide or death (as in the case of Ajax, or Ino and Procne;[1] see Medea's own earlier courageous resolve to face death at 393), Medea further destroys the heroic integrity of her ethic. Unlike the Sophoclean hero who gains a certain authority not only by dying but by remaining tragically alienated from the world to the bitter end, the once mistreated and misunderstood Medea goes off to fit all too well into the contemporary world; indeed, she will very likely marry Aegeus and go on, after denying progeny to Jason, to produce the child Medus.[2] Medea's final transformation into an amoral deity, something beyond the human female or male, expresses not only the death and betrayal of her maternal self[3] but what she has become through her abuse of her masculine ethic. Unlike Sophocles in the *Ajax,* with its concluding recognition of the hero's epic glory despite his earlier brutality and dehumanization, Euripides seems finally to have little nostalgia for the epic past. Indeed, we might view the play as—at least in part—an implicit attack on the typical Sophoclean hero. But, above all, the poet comes close to labeling the "friends-enemies" ethic as destructive of humanity and human values and thus suitable only for gods.

In his long career Euripides created adulterous and murderous women, as well as male characters, like Jason here (esp. 573–75) or Hippolytus (*Hippolytus* 616–68), who indulge in misogynistic outbursts. He also created courageous female sacrificial victims, female advocates of public ideals, defenders of the female sex like Melanippe, and a Helen who sat out the Trojan War guarding her virtue in Egypt. Aristophanes' accusation of misogyny in *Thesmophoriazasue* must be viewed in relation to that poet's own (mis)representations of women;

8. Deceptiveness is, of course, also thought to be a typically feminine vice, and Odysseus' heroism had become suspect by the fifth century.
9. Bongle 1977: 32, 50, and 55 tends to view Medea's excessive pursuit of her code in terms that better suit the Sophoclean hero.
1. See Mills 1980: 289–96, on the similarities and differences between Ino and Procne's story and Medea's, which includes a supernatural dimension. Newton 1985: 501–2 speculates that if, as seems likely, Euripides invented Ino's killing of her children, Medea's crime truly lacks precedent.
2. In other versions (although this one was certainly known in Attic tragedy) Medus was the son of a barbarian king whom Medea married after she fled from Athens. For a discussion and ancient sources, see Graf 1997: 37 and Sfyoeras 1995: esp. 127 n. 9, who stresses the importance of Medea's future in Athens for the interpretation of the Aegeus scene and the play as a whole; he argues that Jason makes Medea into a symbolic (wicked) stepmother like Ino. Burnett 1998: 224 n. 30 is appropriately cautious on the status of Medea's myth in Athens at this period.
3. See Schlesinger 1966: 51. In her 1976 Stanford dissertation, Suzanne Mills, noting the similarities established between Medea and her rival, the princess, intriguingly suggests that Medea moves toward divinity through the sacrifice of a double.

besides, his Euripides is finally exonerated on the basis of his *Helen* and *Andromeda*.[4] Knox argues that *Medea* is neither feminist nor misogynist but a play about the wrongs done to and by women.[5] *Medea* exposes male suppression of women in marriage and the tragic results of a male refusal to recognize in women the capacities, feelings, and needs that they accept for themselves; and it shows the corrupting effects of this mistreatment on a woman of tremendous feeling and intelligence.[6] At the same time Medea's overly literal imitation of an anachronistic masculine code, her dehumanization, and her betrayal of her own sex could be said equally to confirm woman's ultimate incapacity for independence and civilized behavior. For if Euripides is using Medea to examine critically masculine heroism and masculine ethics, he cannot be arguing that women should be liberated to pursue these same goals, and there is a certain irony in the heroine's pursuit of a code that even Sophocles' *Ajax* displayed as politically if not emotionally outmoded.

Yet this play is equally about the wrongs done to and by men. By showing how Medea's concern for status and revenge at all costs can disintegrate into something uncomfortably close to the callous utilitarianism of Jason and destroy those whom her ideals were meant to protect, Euripides makes a devastating philosophical case against both the shallow modern ethics of Jason and Creon and the heroic ethics of the archaic past. Only Athens, with its harmonious blend of *erōs* and *sophia*, and Aegeus, who shows respect both for Medea's person and for her oaths, appear exempt from the general indictment; yet Athens itself is about to be visited by Medea. Medea seems to make at first an eloquent case for her own truth, integrity, and justice. Yet in the end her inability to trust her own maternal voice in the monologue destroys any hopes for a more enlightened form of human ethics, for the creation of an authoritative female identity and integrity that could contest masculine ethics, whether archaic or contemporary. By dividing Medea's self along sexual lines, Euripides creates, not a private psychological drama and/or an abstract struggle between reason and passion, but an ambiguous inquiry into the relation between human ethics and social structure.

*   *   *

4. See Zeitlin 1981: 186–94.
5. See Knox 1977: 211 and also Reckford 1968: 339–40.
6. Gill 1996 offers a valuable expansion of this point. In his view, Medea's infanticide is an exemplary, reasoned response to Jason's refusal, especially in their first debate, to recognize their mutual responsibility to their relationship (marriage as an ethical partnership), her past favors to Jason, the legitimacy of her complaints, and her status as a fully human agent.

WORKS CITED

Barlow, Shirley. 1989. "Stereotype and Reversal in Euripides' *Medea*." *Greece & Rome* 36:2: 158–71.

———. 1995. "Euripides' *Medea*: A Subversive Play." In *Stage Directions: Essays in Honor of E. W. Handley*, ed. Alan Griffiths. London: Institute of Classical Studies, 36–45.

Boedeker, Deborah. 1991. "Euripides' *Medea* and the Vanity of LOGOI." *Classical Philology* 86: 95–112.

Bongie, Elizabeth Bryson. 1977. "Heroic Elements in the *Medea* of Euripides." *Transactions and Proceedings of the American Philological Association* 107: 27–56.

Burnett, Anne Pippin. 1973. "*Medea* and the Tragedy of Revenge." *Classical Philology* 68: 1–24.

———. 1998. *Revenge in Attic and Later Tragedy*. Berkeley: U of California P.

Buttrey, T. V. 1958. "Accident and Design in Euripides' Medea." *American Journal of Philology* 79: 1–17.

Collinge, N. E. 1962. "Medea *ex Machina*." *Classical Philology* 57: 151–60.

Cunningham, Maurice P. 1954. "Medea *apo mechanes*." *Classical Philology* 49: 151–60.

Easterling, P. E. 1977. "The Infanticide in Euripides' *Medea*." *Yale Classical Studies* 25: 177–91.

Flory, Stewart. 1978. "Medea's Right Hand: Promises and Revenge." *Transactions and Proceedings of the American Philological Association* 108: 69–74.

Fortenbaugh, William W. 1970. "On the Antecedents of Aristotle's Bipartite Psychology." *Greek, Roman and Byzantine Studies* 11: 233–50.

Friedrich, Rainer. 1993. "Medea *apolis*: On Euripides' Dramatization of the Crisis of the Polis." In *Tragedy, Comedy, and the Polis*, ed. Alan H. Sommerstein, Stephen Halliwell, Jeffrey Henderson, and Bernhard Zimmermann. Bari: Levante, 219–39.

Galis, Leon. 1992. "Medea's Metamorphosis." *Eranos* 90: 65–81.

Gellie, George. 1988. "The Character of Medea." *Bulletin of the Institute of Classical Studies* 35: 15–22.

Gill, Chris. 1987. "Two Monologues of Self-Division: Euripides *Medea* 1021–80 and Seneca *Medea* 893–977." In *Homo Viator: Classical Essays for John Bramble*, ed. Michael Whitby, Philip R. Hardie, and Mary Whitby. Bristol: Bristol Classical Press, 25–37.

———. 1996. *Personality in Greek Epic, Tragedy, and Philosophy: The Self in Dialogue*. Oxford: Oxford UP.

Gould, John. 1978. "Dramatic Character and Human Intelligibility." *Proceedings of the Cambridge Philological Society* 24: 43–63.

Graf, Fritz. 1997. "Medea, the Enchantress from Afar: Remarks on a Well-Known Myth." In *Medea: Essays on Medea in Myth, Literature, and Philosophy*, ed. James J. Clauss and Sarah Iles Johnston. Princeton: Princeton UP, 21–43.

Gredley, Bernard. 1987. "The Place and Time of Victory: Euripides' *Medea*." *Bulletin of the Institute of Classical Studies* 34: 27–39.

Harder, Ruth E. 1993. *Die Frauenrollen bei Euripides*. Stuttgart: M & P.

Knox, B. M. W. 1977. "The *Medea* of Euripides." *Yale Classical Studies* 25: 193–225.

Loraux, Nicole. 1987. *Tragic Ways of Killing a Woman*. Trans. Anthony Forster. Cambridge, MA: Harvard UP.

Manuwald, B. 1983. "Der Mord an den Kindern: Bemerkungen zu den Medea-Tragödien des Euripides und des Neophron." *Wiener Studien* 17: 27–61.

McDermott, Emily A. 1989. *Euripides' Medea: The Incarnation of Disorder*. University Park, PA: Penn State UP.

Michelini, Ann N. 1989. "Neophron and Euripides' *Medea* 1056–80." *Transactions and Proceedings of the American Philological Association* 119: 115–35.

Mills, Sophie. 1980. "The Sorrows of Medea." *Classical Philology* 75: 289–96.

Newton, Rick M. 1985. "Ino in Euripides' *Medea*." *American Journal of Philology* 106: 496–502.

Ohlander, Stephen. 1989. *Dramatic Suspense in Euripides' and Seneca's Medea*. New York: Peter Lang.

Paduano, Guido. 1968. *La fomazione del mundo ideologico e poetico di Euripide*. Pisa: Nistri-Lischi.

Page, Denys. [1938] 1971. *Medea*. Oxford: Oxford UP.

Pucci, Pietro. 1980. *The Violence of Pity in Euripides' Medea*. Ithaca: Cornell UP.

Rabinowitz, Nancy Sorkin. 1993. *Anxiety Veiled: Euripides and the Traffic in Women*. Ithaca: Cornell UP.

Reckford, Kenneth J. 1968. "Medea's First Exit." *Transactions and Proceedings of the American Philological Association* 99: 329–59.

Rehm, Rush. 1989. "Medea and the Logos of the Heroic." *Eranos* 87: 97–115.

Rohdich, Hermann. 1968. *Die Euripideische Tragödie*. Heidelberg: Carl Winter.

Schein, Seth L. 1990. "*Philia* in Euripides' *Medea*." In *Cabinet of the Muses: Essays on Classical and Comparative Literature in Honor of Thomas G. Rosenmeyer*, ed. Mark Griffith and Donald J. Mastronarde. Berkeley: U of California P, 57–73.

Schlesinger, Eilhard. 1966. "Zu Euripides' Medea." *Hermes* 94: 26–53.

Segal, Charles P. 1996. "Euripides' *Medea*: Vengeance, Reversal, and Closure." *Pallas* 45: 15–54.

Seidensticker, Bernd. 1995. "Women on the Tragic Stage." In *History, Tragedy, Theory: Dialogues on Athenian Drama*, ed. Barbara Goff. Austin TX: U of Texas P, 151–73.

Sfyoeras, Pavlos. 1995. "The Ironies of Salvation: The Aigeus Scene in Euripides' *Medea*." *Classical Journal* 90: 125–42.

Strohm, Hans. 1957. *Euripides*. Munich: C.H. Beck.

Visser, Margaret. 1986. "Medea: Daughter, Sister, Wife, Mother— Natal Family versus Conjugal Family in Greek and Roman Myths about Women." In *Greek Tragedy and Its Legacy*, ed. Martin Cropp, Elaine Fantham, and S. E. Scully. Calgary: Calgary UP, 149–66.

von Fritz, Kurt. 1962. *Antike und Modern Tragödie*. Berlin: De Gruyter.

Walsh, George B. 1979. "Public and Private in Three Plays of Euripides." *Classical Philology* 74: 294–309.

Williamson, Margaret. 1985. "A Woman's Place in Euripides' *Medea*." *Joint Association of Classical Teachers' Review* 3: 16–20. Revised in *Euripides, Women and Sexuality*, ed. Anton Powell. New York: Routledge, 16–31.

Wolff, Christian. 1982. "Euripides." In *Ancient Writers: Greece and Rome*, ed. T. J. Luce. New York: Scribner's, 233–65.

Worthington, Ian. 1990. "The Ending of Euripides' *Medea*." *Hermes* 118: 502–505.

Zeitlin, Froma. 1981. "Travesties of Gender and Genre in Aristophanes' *Thesmophoriazusae*." In *Reflections of Women in Antiquity*, ed. Helene P. Foley. New York: Gordon and Breach, 186–217. Revised in *Playing the Other: Gender and Society in Classical Greek Civilization*. 1996. Chicago: U of Chicago P, 375–416.

EDITH HALL

Divine and Human in Euripides' *Medea*†

At the climax of Euripides' *Medea*, the voices of the Colchian sorceress' two young boys, inside their house with their mother, are heard screaming for help from backstage. But then they fall silent. Jason arrives at his former residence in Corinth and demands that the doors be opened. Like Jason and the chorus, we have every reason to believe Medea is inside, with the slaughtered children. We actually saw her enter the house just a few minutes previously, stating unambiguously in her last speech that she was going to kill them,

† From *Looking at Medea: Essays and a Translation of Euripides' Tragedy*, ed. David Stuttard (London: Bloomsbury, 2014), pp. 139–55. Copyright © Edith Hall 2014. Reprinted by permission of Bloomsbury Academic, an imprint of Bloomsbury Publishing Plc.

with a sword, without further delay. Our experience of Greek tragedy leads us to expect that the doors will open, and on the wheeled
platform called the *ekkyklema*, or 'rolling-out machine', a terrible
tableau will come into view—Medea, covered in blood, bestriding
the corpses of her little ones with a gore-streaked weapon in her
hands. As Jason bangs at the doors, physically trying to force them
open, our eyes are therefore concentrated on the level of the entrance
represented by the staging. We expect the house to open and reveal
the scene of carnage inside. Yet nothing happens on this level of
view: instead, it is only on the upper periphery of our vision that the
swinging stage crane at first comes to our attention, with Medea and
the two little corpses visible within.

In Greek tragedy, ordinary mortals do not pass from the interior
of houses to the sky without using doors and without our noticing
it. Nor do they travel by the supernatural means represented by the
machine for the gods. We now know that Medea, for all her plau-
sible emotional anguish and ability to talk in an astonishingly frank
and accessible way to ordinary Corinthian women, is superhuman.
Aristotle, who explained tragedy entirely in terms of human ethics
and psychology rather than theology, sensed that this '*ex machina*'
scene was completely anomalous if Medea is understood to be an
ordinary mortal woman; he therefore objected to the 'inorganic' and
'improbable' ending of the play (*Poetics*, 15, 1454b):

> The denouements of plots ought to arise just from the imitation
> of character, and not from a contrivance, a *deus ex machina*, as
> in *Medea*. The contrivance should be used instead for things out-
> side the play, either all that happened beforehand that a human
> being could not know, or all that happens later and needs fore-
> telling and reporting, for we attribute omnisciene to the gods.

Aristotle is quite explicit that the sort of omniscience which Medea
seems to possess at the end of the play, when she can predict the
moment and manner of Jason's death, belongs not to humans but to
gods.

After the final, vitriolic quarrel between Medea in the chariot and
Jason on the earth, the murderous heroine nevertheless flies off, as
the vindictive Aphrodite disappears from the stage in *Hippolytus* and
Dionysus vanishes at the end of *Bacchae*. Her crime, like a god's
action against a mortal, will remain unpunished, and she gloats over
her possession of the precious corpses. The chorus are stunned: this
is how they conclude their day outside that tragic household in
Corinth (1415–19):

> Zeus on Olympus dispenses many things.
> Gods often contradict our fondest expectations.

What we anticipate does not come to pass.
What we don't expect some god finds a way to make happen.

They are trying to make sense of the horrifying events they have witnessed, from a religious point of view. They need to assume that unseen, supernatural factors or agents, such as gods, have been at work—factors beyond the material, physical world. This is the realm of the unseen and the divine which the Greeks called 'beyond the physical'—'metaphysical'. And this chorus are thoroughly metaphysically *confused*. They are not even sure exactly which god has brought about the events that have just taken place, and insist that they had no way of anticipating the tragedy at all. 'Gods often contradict our fondest expectations.' The Corinthian women's metaphysical incomprehension is important and not atypical of tragedy, a genre in which bafflement is a characteristic philosophical attitude of both staged sufferer and watching spectator.[1] We, too, are fundamentally perplexed, even bewildered, by what happens to Medea and Jason's sons. Can the gods really have intended the terrible deaths that have just occurred to take place? If so, why? Indeed, all the characters in the play, except for Medea, are left either dead or bemused.

Medea is one of the most adapted and performed of all ancient dramas. It has been turned into operas, dance theatre, novels and films as well as new plays. It has proved to be one of the most readily transferable of all the Greek dramas to different religious and cultural contexts. There have been Roman Catholic Medeas, Protestant Medeas, Jewish Medeas, Australian aboriginal Medeas, Japanese Buddhist/Shinto Medeas, Hindu Medeas, Confucian and Dialectical Materialist Medeas.[2] *Medea* is a tragedy that can speak to every community within the global village, and through performances and adaptations has already spoken to more of them, probably, than any other ancient Greek play, except Sophocles' *Oedipus* and *Antigone*. There are several reasons why it has proved so endlessly enduring. They include its focus on conflict between the sexes, its staging of dialogues between individuals of different ethnicity, and its psychological exploration of the ambivalent feelings that children can arouse in a mother. It is also, importantly, an extraordinary exploration of the mind of a murderer, in the process of working herself up to kill another human, which raises timeless legal questions about premeditation, provocation and diminished responsibility.[3] But a

1. Buxton (1988) 41–51.
2. For discussions of some of them, see Hall, Macintosh and Taplin (2000), Rubino (2000), Bätzner, Dreyer and Fischer-Lichte (2010), Biglieri (2005), Lorenzi (2008), Eichelmann (2010), Yixu (2009), Adriani (2006), Nissim and Preda (2006), Behrendt (2007). Unusual adaptations of *Medea* are discussed in several of the essays in both Hall, Macintosh and Wrigley (2004), and Hall and Harrop (2010).
3. Hall (2010b) Ch. 4.

neglected reason why *Medea* is still so powerful is that it asks more metaphysical questions than it answers, even though its theology throughout is basically that of Olympian polytheism. The play leaves problematically *open* the question of the true religious or cosmic purpose of the events it has portrayed.

This inherent metaphysical openness has, in turn, allowed the play to be rewritten and performed in infinite different cultural and religious contexts without ever losing its basic intellectual power. Medea's children continue to scream for help as they die backstage, with the community powerless to help them. Jason's irresponsibility and selfishness continue to be repaid by the disproportionate punishment of multiple bereavements. A completely innocent teenage girl, Creon's daughter, continues to die in agony because she is marrying the man her father has approved. Medea herself, however mysterious she turns out to be, continues to lose her beloved children because her anger is too great to contain. Two entire families—Medea's and the Corinthian royal family—continue to be destroyed, by a terrifying female figure who claims to be implementing the will of the gods, and seems to be unaccountable. Human helplessness in the face of arbitrary and dreadful suffering never received a more compelling dramatization.

An enquiry into the metaphysics of the tragedy and their instrumentality in its cultural stamina needs to look, first, at how the characters in the play themselves explain in religious terms what they are doing and suffering. The most prominent god in the play by far is the supreme ruler of gods and men, Olympian Zeus himself. Zeus supervised the implementation of the rules which constituted Greek popular ethics, and in this capacity was worshipped in a similar way all over the Greek world, by both men and women. His primary assistants in this awesome task were his one-time consort or daughter, Themis (whose name means 'The Right [way of doing things]' or 'Natural Law'), and his daughter, Dikē ('Justice'). The 'rules', which Zeus oversaw, regulated human relationships at every level. They forbade incest, kin-killing, harming suppliants, hosts or guests, failure to bury the dead and perjury. Sometimes they were called 'the unwritten laws' or the 'laws of all the Greeks'. Traditionally-minded Greeks believed that, if they committed any of these crimes, then Zeus might blast them with a thunderbolt or exact retribution another way, often with the assistance of Themis or Dikē. In *Medea* the theology of the play as understood by the nurse, the chorus, and Medea, is on one level, and at the opening of the play, remarkably simple: Jason has broken his marriage vows, the promises he swore to Medea, and has therefore made himself vulnerable as a perjurer to the 'Justice of Zeus'. There was even a special title for Zeus in his capacity as superintendent of oaths, and that was Zeus *Horkios*. The theology of the play is very traditional, and the key divinity is Zeus in his capacity as *Horkios*, along with his designated partner in oath-protection, Themis, and the elemental gods Earth and Sun, by whom oaths were conventionally sworn and who were named as witnesses to them.

The nurse says that Medea is calling on 'Themis, who hears our prayers, and Zeus, who guards the promises men swear' (168–70). The chorus intuitively feel that a woman whose husband has broken his oaths will be protected by Zeus (158–9), and state that Medea calls on Themis (208–10):

> Daughter of Zeus, goddess of the oaths,
> Which carried her across the ocean
> To Hellas, through the dark briny sea.

Indeed, when Medea gloats at the stricken father of her children from the safety of her chariot, she reaffirms that 'Father Zeus' knows what has really passed between them (1352–3), and asks what god would listen to 'a man who doesn't keep his promises, a man who deceives and lies to strangers?' (1391–2).[4]

The play, then, in one sense, is a simple parable of perjury punished. Yet its theology also involves cults that were specifically associated with Corinth and its surrounding areas. Jason owes his safety, he claims, solely to the patronage of the goddess Aphrodite (527). Aphrodite and her son, Eros, are of course thematically relevant to the play, because Medea originally abandoned her homeland and took to crime in order to follow the man with whom she had fallen hopelessly in love. But it will have been just as relevant to Euripides' audience that Aphrodite was also the most important god at Corinth, and the chorus of Corinthian women sing an ode to her (627–41). The temple of Aphrodite at Corinth stood high on the rocky 'Acrocorinth', the hill which towered over the city. By the time of Pindar (that is, before Euripides), there were many maidens serving the goddess in the temple, and the city was famous for its prostitutes, who may have plied their trade in direct connection with Aphrodite's cult. Corinth, which had a steamy reputation, was the perfect setting for a tragedy about sexual jealousy.

Even more significantly, at the end of the play Medea says she is flying off to Athens via the cult centre of Hera Akraia, across the Corinthian gulf at Perachora (one of the wealthiest sanctuaries ever to have been excavated in Greece). She will bury the boys and thereby found a Corinthian ritual (1378–83), which will atone in perpetuity for their deaths. The Doric temple of Hera Akraia, which can still be visited, was ancient and spectacularly adorned with marble tiles; everyone in Euripides' audience will have known of it. Moreover, the large number of votive objects that have been found there by

4. Kovacs (1993) 45–70.

archaeologists (amulets worn by pregnant women, and figurines) show that it was visited by individuals anxious about the health of babies and young children.[5] The killing of Medea's children was therefore presented by the tragedy as the 'charter' or 'foundation' myth for a specific set of cult practices in the Corinthian area. Greek myth and religion often exhibit this 'dialectical' tendency, where opposites are united in the same figures: seers like Teiresias are blind, and children, who have been destroyed, are here somehow to protect other children from destruction.

All over the Greek world, Hera was the deity who represented women's social status as respected wives. Hera was worshipped as Hera *Nympheuomene* (Hera the Bride), Hera *Chera* (Hera the Widow), but also as Hera *Teleia*, Hera the Fulfilled or Fulfiller, the goddess who helped women finalize their marriages satisfactorily with the production of a healthy son. She is, in addition, the angry wife of Zeus, permanently disgruntled at his infidelities. In both capacities—Hera *Teleia* and Hera humiliated by her husband's straying—she is a figure who offers a parallel to Medea in a less specifically Corinthian way. But a discussion of the religion in this play is not complete without Medea's special relationships with two other gods, on the first of whom she calls when no men are in earshot (395–8):

> By Hecate, the goddess
> I worship more than all the others,
> The one I choose to help me in this work,
> Who lives with me deep inside my home,
> These people won't bring pain into my heart
> And laugh about it . . .

It was as a result of this passage that Hecate came to dominate ancient literature's scenes of female witchcraft. Greek lyric poets had already presented her as the dark daughter of Night, the bearer of flaming torches, with some special association with sexual desire implied by making her an attendant of Aphrodite. In art, she is often associated with the huntress Artemis, but in an underworld form, followed by the triple-headed hound of Hell, Cerberus, rather than the hunting dogs who attend Artemis in sunlit glades. But Medea's statement, that Hecate is her favourite goddess, fed the ancient literary imagination. By the time of the third book of *Argonautica*, Apollonius' epic on the Argonauts two centuries later, Medea is imagined to have been a full-time priestess serving in the temple of Hecate in Colchis by the Black Sea; Hecate has taught her how to use magical herbs, which can put out fire, stop rivers in full flow and change the movements of the stars and moon. But Euripides' portrayal of Medea in

5. Baumbach (2004); Johnston (1997) 44–70.

431 BC was exploiting the *real* anxieties of Athenian men, who feared women with expertise in lotions, potions and incantations. This is shown by the evidence relating to the real-life fourth-century trial of a woman named Theoris, who was executed, along with her whole family, for the use of 'drugs and incantations.'[6] A speech by the sophist Antiphon survives from the fifth century, in which a young man accuses his stepmother of murdering his father with poison, and the speaker is clearly able to exploit a strong social stereotype associating female guile with pharmaceutical expertise.

After invoking Hecate, the goddess 'deep inside her home', Medea continues her crucial self-address like this (401–6):

> So come, Medea,
> call on all those things you know so well,
> as you plan this and set it up. Let the work,
> this deadly business, start. It's a test of wills.
> You see what you have to put up with.
> You must not let Jason's marriage make you
> a laughing stock among Corinthians,
> compatriots of Sisyphus, for you
> trace your family from a noble father
> and from Helios, the Sun. So get to work.

Medea's other special relationship is with her grandfather Helios, who, indeed, lends her the chariot in which she can escape at the end of the play. The Sun is also invoked by Aegeus, when he swears his oath to Medea, as it is by many other oath-takers in Greek tragedy, and this reflects standard practice; the regular divinities invoked in oaths, as we have noted, were Zeus, the Earth and the Sun.

Helios is actually a rather difficult god to grasp, at least as early in antiquity as this, when in most places in Greece he does not seem to have been particularly important, and it is not yet clear that he has been firmly identified with Apollo. It is from much later antiquity that his connection with Corinth is implied by the eleven slabs with mask-like heads of Helios which have been excavated in the Corinthian Odeum; these may actually have decorated the *scaenae frons* (facing of the stage building). Helios had a major cult in rather few Greek communities, the most important, of course, being on Rhodes, where a spectacular sacrifice took place: a team of four horses and a chariot were made to crash into the sea. The myth of Phaethon—which Euripides himself staged in a famous tragedy—may be related to this ritual.[7] An Athenian audience in 431 BC will have been reminded of the Helios on the newly completed east Parthenon pediments (now in

6. See the speech *Against Aristogeiton*, attributed to Demosthenes (25.79–80), and Collins (2001) 477–93.
7. Burkert (1987) 175.

the British Museum), riding with his team of horses from the waves. But Helios was not very significant in Athenian religion in Euripides' day, and the epigraphic evidence for Helios being honoured in cult there, even in a minor role, does not occur until the early fourth century (IG II, 2 4962). Helios seems to have been associated with the growth of crops, and was connected with the festival of Thargelia, held in May, when the first cereals and fruits were ripe. Passages in Plato imply that those Athenians who paid the Sun/Helios special respect, in the fifth century at least, were regarded as rather avant-garde and odd, if not actually outlandish and barbarian. After all, in Aristophanes' *Peace* (421 BC) we are told that Helios and Selene (the Moon) are betraying Hellas to the barbarians (406ff.) and the reason the hero Trygaeus gives is that 'we sacrifice to the Olympians, but barbarians sacrifice to *them*'.

Medea, therefore, has rather offbeat divine associates in Hecate and Helios. She is not exactly a goddess, but neither is she suscep-tible to most of the constraints of mortality—she can physically escape what, for a mortal woman, would now be certain death at the hands of Jason and the Corinthians, and she can fly in a super-natural vehicle; what is more, there is no known ancient tradition, in any Greek or Roman author, that she ever died. 'Witch' is far too weak a term for her; she sees herself as the agent of Zeus' justice, and, as some sort of demigod, she never reveals exactly what goes on when she is communing with Hecate and Helios. No wonder the chorus, and the audience, end the play so baffled.

The play, therefore, is paradoxically both traditional and extremely peculiar in its metaphysics. It offers a relatively simple explanation of the role of the major gods in the action: Jason is punished by Zeus *Horkios*, through Medea, for perjury; Corinth is the kind of place where sex becomes an issue, especially in the case of a man already patronized by Aphrodite; the events are a theological explanation for the origins of rituals at the cult of Hera Akraia. But Medea herself destabilizes this simple explanation. At first one of Euripides' appar-ently most accessible heroines, who speaks in ways that can seem astonishingly direct and immediate even today, she turns out to have been completely unknowable all along. She has not been playing the game of life according to the ethical rules understood or decipher-able by humans at all.

Perhaps the most important theological moment in the play occurs at the point where Medea makes up her mind to kill the children. After the scene with Aegeus, she calls out, triumphantly (764–6):

> Oh Zeus, and Justice, child of Zeus,
> and flaming Helios—now, *my friends*,
> we'll triumph over all my enemies.

Medea, astonishingly, counts amongst her 'friends' and allies not only Helios and Justice, but the top Olympian god, Zeus himself. The chorus hear this strange note that she strikes, and respond in what are the most telling lines, perhaps, in the whole play (811–13):

> Since you've shared your plans with me, I urge you not
>   to do this.
> I want to help you, holding to the standards of *human* law.

The chorus are, in fact, articulating a view consonant with the contemporary agnostic political theorist and philosopher, Protagoras, who insisted that humans had only their own powers of observation and reasoning to rely on in looking for explanations of events and phenomena. He famously said:

> About the gods, I am not able to know whether they exist or do not exist, nor what they are like in form; for the factors preventing knowledge are many: the obscurity of the subject, and the shortness of human life.[8]

The chorus are insisting, quite rightly, that *human* law does not sanction the murder of children in punishment of oath-breaking husbands. Medea, on the other hand, instantiates the philosophical principle underlying the whole play—that human reason is *not* a sufficient resource for ensuring happiness, since life is uncontrollable, disaster is unavoidable, the principles driving the universe are inscrutable, and suffering is indiscriminate and unfair. Most people who attend a production of *Medea* today do not think very hard about the role of the gods, if they think about them at all. But they still feel just as powerfully the philosophical bewilderment that Medea's role arouses. This is surely an important explanation for the translatability of the tragedy into every cultural and religious tradition that has performed it in the global village.

In the European Renaissance, the Euripidean Greek *Medea* was rediscovered, and began to be read alongside the Senecan version, which was more accessible because it was in the more widely understood Latin language. Seneca had reacted to the metaphysical bafflement which Medea inspired, in all who watched her on stage or heard about her in epic poetry, by making her summon the help of what feels at the time like half the divinities in the pantheon. This is his Medea's opening imprecation (1–12):

> You, gods of wedlock and you,
> Juno Lucina of the wedding bed,
> And you, Minerva, who taught Tiphys

---

8. Protagoras Fragment 1 Diels-Kranz.

To conquer seas in his new craft,
And you, cruel ruler of the deep Ocean,
and Titan, who shares out daylight to the world,
and you, triple-bodied Hecate, whose shining countenance
ratifies the silent rites of the mysteries,
and whichever of the gods Jason swore his oaths to me by—
gods to whom Medea may appeal more lawfully than he did—
and Chaos of eternal Night, realms remote from the gods,
    Unhallowed Ghosts
and Lord of the kingdom of despair, with your Queen,
    abducted by force . . .

Some of these gods are culturally 'translated' into their Roman ava-
tars from the Euripidean Medea's own speeches—thus Hera
becomes Juno Lucina, Helios becomes Titan and Hecate remains
Hecate. But Seneca's Medea adds and names other gods altogether.
They include 'gods of wedlock' (presumably Hymen), Minerva
(because she helped make the *Argo* and supported its helmsman),
Ocean, Night, the ghosts of the unburied, Pluto and Proserpina.
Seneca's Medea then explicitly summons to her side the 'Furies who
avenge crime, Furies with loose unkempt hair, writhing with snakes,
and clutching the smoking torches in your gory hands' (13–15). If
they compared Euripides' heroine with Seneca's, and her liberally
invoked divine assistance, new dramatists attempting a play about
Medea must have felt even more confused. They will have been further perturbed by the newly philosophical tone of Seneca's Jason.
Seneca, being a Stoic, was not fully satisfied with such a god-centred
explanation of Medea's crime, either: something closer to his own
philosophical position on her crimes may underlie the final lines of
the play, in which Jason tells Medea to be gone to the furthest
regions of the universe as understood in the physics as well as the
metaphysics of the Stoic and Epicurean schools of philosophy:
'Travel on, then, through the lofty spaces of high heaven and bear
witness, where you ride, that there are no gods!' (1026–7). If the
Roman dramatist could so drastically amplify, supplement and
rewrite the religious and philosophical dimension of Medea's story,
no wonder much later playwrights felt that they had every right to
make it comprehensible to their own, very different, audiences.

    By the eighteenth century, Euripides' play, as well as Seneca's, had
become increasingly familiar through translation into modern languages and adaptation for performance. Christianized neoclassical
Medeas were the eighteenth-century norm in spoken theatre. The
horror of the intentional child-killing needed to be ameliorated for
an audience with strong ideals of femininity and equally strong
Christian beliefs. One way of making Medea acceptable was to allow

her exculpating fits of madness in which she committed her murders, as Agave in *Bacchae* is deranged when she kills her son Pentheus, or Heracles is psychotically deluded when he commits triple filicide in *Heracles Mainomenos*. In Richard Glover's *Medea*, performed in London at Drury Lane in 1767, for example, a good deal of emphasis was given to Medea's temporary madness or 'phrenzy'. Another strategy was to bestow an altruistic motivation upon Medea, for example, that the Corinthians would kill them by a much worse death if she did not kill them quickly herself. This was the expedient selected by Ernest Legouvé for his popular *Médée*, much performed after its 1857 premiere in Paris.[9] In more recent times, adaptors and theatre directors have adopted several different strategies for dealing with the play's pagan religion. The first strategy has been wholesale *deletion*—many adaptations and stagings of *Medea* simply omit many of the references to the gods, certainly to the more obscure figures such as Themis and Dikē The specific references to Zeus and Hera often become rephrased as vague reference to 'god' or 'gods' or 'heaven', adaptable to almost any cultural context. More importantly, very few productions suggest in the final scene that Medea is perhaps not a human, after all.

Since the early twentieth century, the chief strategy used to make the religion in *Medea* comprehensible to theatre audiences has, however, been allegory. 'The gods' have been made to stand for something else, for another force of immense destructive potential, which is not fully comprehended or controllable by humans, any more than the chorus of Euripides' *Medea* understand her or can control her actions, when she claims that 'Zeus and Justice' are her allies. One of the first productions to allegorize the chariot scene was also the first in a translation (rather than adaptation) into the English language. This production, directed by Harley Granville-Barker in London in 1907, was very important in cultural history because of its connection with the movement for women's equality in the United Kingdom.[1]

The translation was by the Oxford Greek scholar Gilbert Murray, who had supported the women's suffrage movement since 1889. Murray and Barker may have been influenced by the success of Max Reinhardt's Berlin production of *Medea*, in a translation by the famous German classicist Ulrich von Wilamowitz-Moellendorff, in 1904. But the political climate also made *Medea* a significant choice. In 1906 the movement for women's suffrage had been inaugurated, and in 1907 the first mass arrests of suffragettes shocked the public: no fewer than sixty-five served sentences in Holloway Prison. Support for the movement grew rapidly, inspiring Barker to produce

9. See Hall, Macintosh and Taplin (2000); Hall and Macintosh (2005) Ch. 14.
1. See Hall (1999) 42–77.

the first of the whole series of suffrage plays, which flourished on the commercial stage, *Votes for Women*, by the Ibsen-influenced Elizabeth Robins. This impassioned piece staged a suffragette meeting in Trafalgar Square. October 1907 saw the staging at the Royal Court of Mrs W. J. Clifford's dramatic examination of the effects of divorce on women, *Hamilton's Second Marriage*. But it also witnessed the actress Edyth Olive, in the title role of Euripides' *Medea*, emerging from her house in Corinth and lecturing her audience on the injustices suffered by women at the hands of men.

Yet this 1907 suffragette Medea was no divinity. Reviewers remarked on how surprisingly 'human' Medea was, and complimented Olive on winning the audience's sympathy. In a seminal study of Euripides, published in 1913, Gilbert Murray writes about Euripides thus:

> To us he seems an aggressive champion of women; more aggressive, and certainly far more appreciative, than Plato. Songs and speeches from the Medea are recited today at suffragist meetings.[2]

Murray's book has proved perhaps the most influential interpretation of Euripides of all time. But Murray's translation, Harley Granville-Barker's production and Edyth Olive's acting combined to present the theatrical *machina* as a *metaphor*. It symbolized something very real—the scale of the consequences of a man hurting a very *human* woman. Although his translation was fairly conservative—even archaizing—in style and idiom, and kept almost all of the references to specific divinities, in the 'Introduction' Murray saw the ancient gods, and Medea especially, as designed to be read allegorically:

> The truth is that in this play Medea herself is the *dea ex machina*. The woman whom Jason and Creon intended simply to crush has been transformed by her injuries from an individual human being into a sort of living Curse. She is inspired with superhuman force. Her wrongs and her hate fill all the sky. And the judgment pronounced on Jason comes not from any disinterested or peace-making God, but from his own victim transfigured into a devil.

Medea is a hate-filled woman, transformed by her injuries into something almost superhuman—a human victim of male irresponsibility and cruelty transformed by injustice into a daemonic negative force of almost cosmic potency.

Gilbert Murray himself regarded Medea's child-killing as realistic: 'Euripides had apparently observed how common it is, when a

2. Murray (1913) 32.

woman's mind is deranged by suffering, that her madness takes the form of child-murder.'[3] The prominent suffragette Sylvia Pankhurst recalled how the great stirring of social conscience in 1906 had led to economically privileged women noticing the hardships of women in the lower classes. The focus was on a number of tragic cases of poor women, 'which in other days might have passed unnoticed', but were now used to underline women's inferior status:

> Daisy Lord, the young servant sentenced to death for infanticide; Margaret Murphy, the flower-seller, who, after incredible hardships, attempted to poison herself and her ailing youngest child . . . Julia Decies, committed to seven years' penal servitude for throwing vitriol at the man who had betrayed and deserted her; Sarah Savage, imprisoned on the charge of cruelty to her children for whom she had done all that her miserable poverty would permit. By reprieve petitions, by propaganda speeches and articles, the names and the stories of these unfortunates were torn from their obscurity, to be branded upon the history of the women's movement of their day.[4]

The dismal crimes of these modern Medeas—infanticide, violence against their husbands, child abuse—were now seen as caused by their social status. Even intentional child-murder by women was now being seen as connected with male irresponsibility: like Daisy Lord and Margaret Murphy, Medea could now kill her children with premeditation and be given, at least in the progressive theatre, a sympathetic hearing.

Many productions of *Medea* have followed this seminal theatrical event by 'allegorizing' Medea's wrath and superhuman power as the potential reaction of women suffering under a patriarchal social system. This was especially the case in the late 1970s and 1980s, when the Feminist and Women's Rights movements were at the top of the political and cultural agenda, at least in Western Europe and the USA. But in more recent productions, the divine element has often also been 'allegorized' in a psychological way, as representing Medea's disturbed psyche. This was certainly the case, for example, in Deborah Warner's production, starring Fiona Shaw, which was such a commercial hit in both London and New York in 2000–1. There was no sign of any god from the machine; Medea clearly had a mental breakdown, and ended the play in a bizarre dialogue with Jason, washing the blood from her body. Similarly, the 2006 *Medea* at the Deutsches Theater in Berlin, directed by Barbara Frey and

3. Murray (1906) 94.
4. Pankhurst (1931) 225–6.

starring Nina Hoss, was a psychological interpretation, although the
damage to Medea's psyche was clearly caused in part by sexism.
Medea spent most of the play confined inside a box-like house that
represented both her dismal apartment and her inner mental world.
Disturbing images and sounds were experienced by her and the
audience, which seemed to represent the fluctuating pictures and
sensations in her disturbed consciousness, while hands and other
objects protruded inwards from the walls, when her subconscious
or conscious violent impulses were threatening to overwhelm her.

But there has been another way in which the divine element has
been understood over the last half-century, and that is more to do
with post-colonialism than with either feminism or psychoanalysis.
Medea's revenge has very frequently been 'allegorized' as the violence of an oppressed people or ethnic group against their long-
term imperial masters. This is an interesting development, because
before World War II, Medea's religion was often represented precisely as a retrograde, primitive, barbaric belief system, in contrast
with what was presented as the more enlightened, Western, Christianized religion practised by Jason and his countrymen. This pattern can be seen, for example, in the Russian verse tragedy *Georgian
Night* of the 1820s by A. Griboedov, where the Medea figure was a
superstitious pagan Georgian serf-class mother, taking revenge on
her owner with the aid of the *Ali*, malicious female spirits of Georgian paganism. Griboedov almost wilfully ignored the actual offi-
cial Christian status of Georgia in this presentation of the mother
as an atavistic Asiatic barbarian.[5]

* * * Henri-Rene's Lenormand's rewriting of *Medea* as *Asie* in
1931 similarly substituted a Christian religious framework by con-
trasting his Medea-figure's 'heathen' religion with the Christianity
practised by her errant husband's culture. The Indo-Chinese Princess Katha Naham Moun's children have been educated in the
Christian faith by French missionaries, and this has alienated them
from her. De Mezzana (Jason) tells his significantly blonde European Creusa (Aimée) that his marriage was scarcely valid as it was
performed to the sound of tom-toms in the presence of tribal
demons.[6] Only a year later, Maxwell Anderson's *The Wingless Victory* (1932) staged a North American marrying a Malay wife, Aparre.
He comes from strict Puritan family and Creusa's name could not
be more Christian—Faith'. But Aparre comes to realize that she
must carry out the fate that her old religion *dictates* must befall the
children of someone who elopes from her Malaysian culture with
an alien, and that fate is death.[7]

5. See Layton (1992) 195–213.
6. See Macintosh (2005) 65–77.
7. See Belli (1967) 226–39.

In the era of European empires, such an interpretation of Medea's religion as inherently inferior but extremely frightening was frequent. But over the last few decades, the gods, in whom Medea believes, have often been used in anti-colonial and anti-racist productions to symbolize the original, pre-colonial identity and culture of people who have subsequently been subjugated, oppressed, deracinated and transplanted, and therefore as a potentially liberating force. Medea's escape in the machine can become, in such productions, a metaphor for the acquisition of political independence, but with a warning: alongside liberation comes the threat of terrible, violent reprisals against the colonizing power. This was the way in which the religious element in the play was used, for example, in a South African production directed by Mark Fleishman and Jenny Reznek at the Arena Theatre, Cape Town, in 1994.[8] The different cultural and religious backgrounds of the people of South Africa were suggested by the use of different languages including Xhosa and Zulu, as well as English and Afrikaans. The production was 'a timely reminder to South Africans rejoicing in their new freedom that a meeting of different cultures must be managed in a transparently fair and equitable way if disaster is to be avoided';[9] Medea's superhuman quality therefore embodied the potential for catastrophic anarchy to break out in post-apartheid South Africa.

Ethnic and racial resistance are often more or less commensurate, as in racially divided South Africa, with class identity, and it is the threat of class warfare that is the final way in which I want to suggest that Medea's divinity has been allegorized in recent decades. In Latin America, for example, Medea's religion has been a symbol of the suppressed African origins and identity of a large proportion of the population, whose ancestors arrived as slaves in South America centuries ago. A play by Chico Buarque de Hollanda and Paolo Pontes (1985), entitled *Gota d'Água* (*Drop of Water*), relocated the story of Medea to Brazil, and involved the Afro-Brazilian spiritist religions, that date from the arrival of African slaves to Brazil in the sixteenth century. They ultimately derive from Yoruba, the West African religion, but have syncretically assimilated Amerindian and Roman Catholic elements. The most significant one, and the one in which their Medea figure is an expert, is called Umbanda. Since the 1930s, Umbanda's adherents have been closely identified with the poor urban working class and underclass in Brazil. They worship a range of spirits (*orixás*) intermittently identified with Christian saints—Ogum, for example, is St George.[1] The Umbanda religion

8. Well analysed by Yvonne Banning (1999) 42–8.
9. See the review of this production by Betine Van Zyl Smit, available online at www.didaskalia.net/issues/vol1no5/vanzyl.html.
1. See DiPuccio (1990) 1–10.

uses much magical discourse and many spells. The play *Gota d'Água*
pits Creonte's atheist, sceptical, capitalistic rhetoric against the
Medea figure's magical language, and she wins. He is scornful of
her religion and it thus becomes a crucial factor. But the reason is
not that the playwrights are believers—more that the magic becomes
a metaphor for potential ethnic and class resistance.

The Brazilian version of *Medea* devised by de Hollanda and Pontes
is one where Medea's ancient religion represents the anger and potential revenge of people oppressed not only by institutionalized racism,
that goes back centuries, but by their abject position in the economic
and social systems. It is not the spirits of Umbanda who unleash their
terrible violence, through the superhuman Medea, but the wrath of
people humiliated and kept in poverty. The transmission of this kind
of interpretation all over the planet, to Africa, India and Australia as
well as Brazil, is partly a result of the influential film *Medea* of 1969,
directed by Pier Paolo Pasolini and starring Maria Callas. This film
uses Medea's religion in a fascinating way, implying that the sacrifice
of the children is an ancient practice endorsed according to her own
culture in cases of desertion by a husband. Pasolini is certainly influenced here by anti-colonialism and its defence of the rights of all
peoples to religious self-determination. But it is even more important
that he himself saw the religion in *Medea* as a symbol of what was
fundamentally a *political* issue: he saw no difference, he said, between
the fundamental Marxist argument underlying his film *The Gospel
According to St Matthew* (1964) and his *Medea*:

> In reality a director always makes the same film, at least for a
> long period of his life, just as a poet always writes the same
> poem. These are variations, even profound ones, on a single
> theme. And the theme, as always in my films, is a type of ideal
> and ever unresolved relationship between the poor and the com-
> mon world, let's say the sub-proletariat, and the educated,
> middle-class, historical world. This time I have dealt directly
> and explicitly with this theme. Medea is the heroine of a sub-
> proletarian world, an archaic and religious world. Jason is
> instead the hero of a rational, lay, modern world. And their love
> represents the conflict between these two hemispheres. It's an
> old polemic of mine: the centre of the petit bourgeois civilisa-
> tion is reason, while everything that is irrational, for example
> art, challenges bourgeois reason.[2]

Medea worships, and in some ways actually is herself representative
of, the 'archaic' and 'religious' gods, that are also the 'sub-proletariat'.
Jason represents the 'reason', on which the bourgeois ruling class

---

2. See www.filmfestival.gr/tributes/2003-2004/cinemythology/uk/film36.html, a translation of passages from Pasolini's *Le regole di un'illusione* (Rome, 1991).

pride themselves, and with which they have dominated the world. These two groups are in perpetual conflict. Here Medea becomes not only the force that can challenge the ruling class, but a metaphor herself for Art, the 'irrational' medium, which can nevertheless challenge the bourgeoisie's hegemony.

What a long way we have come from the bafflement of the women in Euripides' play, when they realise that Medea is somehow working the will of heaven! The blinding, elemental force of the Euripidean Medea, aloft in her fiery chariot, was, for believers in Olympian religion, a symbol of the terrible things that Fate can deal out to humans who have broken any of the fundamental taboos. In later eras, Medea's existential status as a quasi-god or demi-god has usually been replaced: her strength has sometimes been interpreted as the workings of a character suffering from psychosis, but equally often as a social or political force—the anger of oppressed women, ethnic groups and social underclasses. But, when we approach Euripides' play, it always needs to be remembered, that it is the awesome, unknowable religious element, the metaphysical power embodied in the mysterious figure of Medea, which ultimately underlies all these interpretations.[3]

WORKS CITED

Adriani, Elena. 2006. *Medea: fortuna e metamorfosi di un archetipo*. Padua: Esedra.

Banning, Yvonne. 1999. "Speaking Silences: Images of Cultural Difference and Gender in Fleishman and Reznek's *Medea*." In *South African Theatre As/And Intervention*, ed. Marcia Blumberg and Dennis Walder. Amsterdam and Atlanta: Rodopi, 41–48.

Bätzner, Nike, Matthias Dreyer, Erika Fischer-Lichte, and Astrid Schönhagen, eds. 2010. *Medeamorphosen: Mythos und ästhetische Transformation*. Munich: Fink.

Baumbach, Jens David. 2004. *The Significance of Votive Offerings in Selected Hera Sanctuaries in the Peloponnese, Ionia and Western Greece*. Oxford: Archaeopress.

Behrendt, Larissa. 2007. "Introduction" in *Contemporary Indigenous Plays*. Sydney: Currency Press.

Belli, Angela. 1967. "Lenormand's *Asie* and Anderson's *The Wingless Victory*." *Comparative Literature* 19: 226–39.

Biglieri, Aníbal A. 2005. *Medea en la literatura española medieval*. La Plata: Fundación Decus.

---

3. A shorter and rather different version of part of this article, with less emphasis on the ancient religious and cultic elements, was first delivered as a lecture in Berlin at the Schaubühne am Lehniner Platz in 2009, and published in German as 'Medea als Mysterium im Global Village' in Bätzner, Dreyer and Fischer-Lichte (2010). I am very grateful for helpful suggestions made at that time by Bernd Seidensticker and Erika Fischer-Lichte.

Burkert, Walter. 1987. *Greek Religion: Archaic and Classical*. Cambridge, MA: Harvard UP.

Buxton, R. G. A. 1988. "Bafflement in Greek Tragedy." *Mètis* 3: 41–51.

Collins, Derek. 2001. "Theoris of Lemnos and the Criminalization of Magic in Fourth-Century Athens." *Classical Quarterly* 51: 477–93.

Di Puccio, Denise. 1990. "The Magic of Umbanda in *Gota d'água*," *Luso-Brazilian Review* 27: 1–10.

Eichelmann, Sabine. 2010. *Der Mythos Medea: Sein Weg durch das kulturelle Gedächtnis zu uns*. Marburg: Tectum.

Hall, Edith. 1999. "Medea and British Legislation before the First World War." *Greece & Rome* 46: 42–77.

———. 2010. "Medea and the Mind of the Murderer." In *Unbinding Medea: Interdisciplinary Approaches to a Classical Myth from Antiquity to the 21st Century*, ed. Heike Bartel and Anne Simon. Oxford: Legenda, 16–24.

Hall, Edith, and Stephe Harrup, eds. 2010. *Theorising Performance: Greek Drama, Cultural History and Critical Practice*. London: Bristol Classical Press.

Hall, Edith, and Fiona Macintosh. 2005. *Greek Tragedy and the British Theatre 1660–1914*. Oxford: Oxford University Press.

Hall, Edith, Fiona Macintosh, and Oliver Taplin, eds. 2000. *Medea in Performance 1500–2000*. Oxford: Legenda.

Hall, Edith, Fiona Macintosh, and Amanda Wrigley, eds. 2004. *Dionysus since 69: Greek Tragedy at the Dawn of the Third Millennium*. Oxford: Oxford UP.

Kovacs, David. 1993. "Zeus in Euripides' *Medea*." *American Journal of Philology* 114: 45–70.

Layton, Susan. 1992. "*Eros and Empire* in Russian Literature about Georgia." *Slavic Review* 51: 195–213.

Lorenzi, Adriana. 2008. *Non restate in silenzio: sulle tracce di Medea Colleoni, Virginia Woolf, Emily Dickinson, Dolores Prato Azzurrina, Gianna Manzini, Antonia Pozzi*. Florence: Le Lettere.

Macintosh, Fiona. 2005. "Medea Between the Wars: The Politics of Race and Empire." In *Rebel Women: Staging Ancient Greek Drama Today*, ed. John M. Dillon and S. E. Wilmer. London: Methuen, 65–77.

Murray, Gilbert. 1906. *The Medea of Euripides*. London: G. Allen & Sons.

———. 1913. *Euripides and His Age*. London: Williams and Norgate.

Nissim, Liana, and Alessandra Preda, eds. 2006. *Magia, gelosia, vendetta: il mito di Medea nelle lettere francesi*. Milan: Cisalpino.

Pankhurst, E. Silvia. 1931. *The Suffragette Movement: An Intimate Account of Persons and Ideals*. London: Longmans, Green, and Co.

Yixu, Lü. 2009. *Medea unter den Deutschen: Wandlungen einer literarischen Figur*. Freiburg: Rombach.

Selected Bibliography

ON GREEK TRAGEDY

Csapo, Eric, and William J. Slater. *The Context of Ancient Drama*. Ann Arbor: U of Michigan P, 1994.

Easterling, P. E., ed. *The Cambridge Companion to Greek Tragedy*. Cambridge: Cambridge UP, 1997.

Foley, Helene P. *Female Acts in Greek Tragedy*. Princeton: Princeton UP, 2001.

Goldhill, Simon. *Reading Greek Tragedy*. Cambridge: Cambridge UP, 1996.

Gregory, Justina, ed. *A Companion to Greek Tragedy*. Malden, MA: Blackwell, 2005.

Hall, Edith. *Inventing the Barbarian: Greek Self-Definition Through Tragedy*. Oxford: Oxford UP, 1989.

McClure, Laura. *Spoken Like a Woman: Speech and Gender in Athenian Drama*. Princeton: Princeton UP, 1999.

McClure, Laura, ed. *A Companion to Euripides*. Malden, MA: Wiley-Blackwell, 2017.

Scodel, Ruth. *An Introduction to Greek Tragedy*. Cambridge: Cambridge UP, 2010.

ON THE MEDEA MYTH

Clauss, James J., and Sarah I. Johnston, eds. *Medea: Essays on Medea in Myth, Literature, Philosophy, and Art*. Princeton: Princeton UP, 1997.

Griffiths, Emma. *Medea*. Abingdon: Routledge, 2006.

ON EURIPIDES' PLAY

Allan, William. *Euripides, Medea*. London: Duckworth, 2002.

Boedeker, Deborah. "Becoming Medea: Assimilation in Euripides." In *Medea: Essays on Medea in Myth, Literature, Philosophy, and Art*, ed. James J. Clauss and Sarah I. Johnston. Princeton: Princeton UP, 1997. 127–48.

Easterling, P. E. "The Infanticide in Euripides' *Medea*." *Yale Classical Studies* 25 (1977): 177–91.

Knox, Bernard. "The *Medea* of Euripides." *Yale Classical Studies* 25 (1977): 193–225.

Luschnig, C. A. E. *Granddaughter of the Sun: A Study of Euripides' Medea*. Leiden: Brill, 2007.

Mastronarde, Donald J., ed. *Euripides, Medea*. Cambridge: Cambridge UP, 2002.

Mossman, Judith. *Euripides, Medea: Introduction, Translation, and Commentary*. Oxford: Aris & Phillips, 2011.

Segal, Charles. "Euripides' *Medea*: Vengeance, Reversal, and Closure." *Pallas* 45 (1996): 15–44.

Stuttard, David, ed. *Looking at Medea: Essays and a Translation of Euripides' Tragedy.* London: Bloomsbury, 2014.

Williamson, Margaret. "A Woman's Place in Euripides' *Medea.*" In *Euripides, Women, and Sexuality,* ed. Anton Powell. New York: Routledge, 1990. 16–31.

Zerba, Michelle. "Medea Hypokrites." *Arethusa* 35 (2002): 325–37.

ON THE LATER RECEPTION OF EURIPIDES' PLAY

Bartel, Heike, and Anne Simon, eds. *Unbinding Medea: Interdisciplinary Approaches to a Classical Myth from Antiquity to the 21st Century.* London: Legenda, 2010.

Foley, Helene P. *Reimagining Greek Tragedy on the American Stage.* Berkeley: U of California P, 2012.

Hall, Edith, and Fiona Macintosh. *Greek Tragedy and the British Theatre 1660–1914.* Oxford: Oxford UP, 2005.

Hall, Edith, Fiona Macintosh, and Oliver Taplin, eds. *Medea in Performance, 1500–2000.* London: Legenda, 2000.

Hall, Edith, Fiona Macintosh, and Amanda Wrigley, eds. *Dionysus Since 69: Greek Tragedy at the Dawn of the Third Millennium.* Oxford: Oxford UP, 2004.

Lauriola, Rosanna. "Medea." In *Brill's Companion to the Reception of Euripides,* eds. Rosanna Lauriola and Kyriakos Demetriou. Leiden: Brill, 2015. 377–442.

McDonald, Marianne. *Euripides in Cinema: The Heart Made Visible.* Philadelphia: Centrum, 1983.

Van Zyl Smit, Bettina. "Black Medeas." In *Looking at Medea: Essays and a Translation of Euripides' Tragedy,* ed. David Stuttard. London: Bloomsbury, 2014. 157–66.